Vatican Encounter

Vatican Encounter

Conversations with Archbishop Marcel Lefebvre

by Jose Hanu

Translated by
Emily Schossberger

SHEED ANDREWS AND McMEEL, INC.
Subsidiary of Universal Press Syndicate
KANSAS CITY

Vatican Encounter:
Conversations with Archbishop Marcel Lefebvre
Copyright © 1978 by Sheed Andrews and McMeel, Inc.

All rights reserved. Printed in the United States of America. No part of this book may be used or reproduced in any manner whatsoever without written permission, except in the case of reprints in the context of reviews. For information write Sheed Andrews and McMeel, Inc., Subsidiary of Universal Press Syndicate, 6700 Squibb Road, Mission, Kansas 66202.

First published in French as *Non: Entretiens de José Hanu avec Mgr Lefebvre* © 1977, Editions Stock

Library of Congress Cataloging in Publication Data

Hanu, Jose.
   Vatican Encounter.

   Translation of Non, mais oui, à l'Église catholique et romaine.
   1. Catholic Church—Doctrinal and controversial works—Catholic authors. I. Lefèbvre, Marcel, 1905-   joint author. II. Title.
BX1779.5.H3613   230'.2   78-6626
ISBN 0-8362-3102-3

Contents

FOREWORD

1. "WE ARE NOT REBELS" 1
   At Econe, 3; What Often Is
   Missing Is Courage, 6;
   I Am Not the Head of the
   Traditionalists, 8

2. SON OF AN INDUSTRIALIST
   OF TOURCOING 11
   A Superficial, Even a False,
   Image, 13; Faith and Patriotism,
   15; Severity and Moral Strictness,
   19; I Shall Die a Monarchist, 21;
   Benedictions and Graces, 24; A
   Woman of Exceptional Character,
   26; Death of a Saint, 28

3. ACTION FRANÇAISE QUESTIONED 31
   A Child without Problems, 33; In
   Gold Letters, 37; The French
   Seminary in Rome, 38; The
   Curate of Lomme, 44; The Bishop
   of Dakar, 46; You Either Are a
   Bishop or You Are Not, 51; The
   Island of Fadiouth, 52

4. THE SERMON OF LILLE 59
   Why Not Simply Explain the
   Gospel? 61; The Social Kingdom
   of Our Lord Jesus Christ, 63

5. DEMYTHOLOGIZING VATICAN II 71
   The Pressure of the Mass Media,
   73; A Great Hope Disappointed,
   75; A Dogmatic or a Pastoral
   Council? 78; The Primacy of the
   Pope, 81; About Religious
   Liberty, 83; The Church and the
   Modern World, 85; A Year Later,
   88; The Case of Cardinal Lienart,
   90; Troubling Facts, 94

6. THE FRUITS OF THE COUNCIL 97
   The Beginning, 99; A Time of
   War, 103; Do We Have the
   Right? 105; Catechesis, 107; Hell,
   111; Deceptive Sciences, 112;
   Stimulators or Educators? 115;
   Divorce, 116; The Charismatics,
   120; The Cassock, 123; A
   Revealing Act, 129; Letter of a
   Dissatisfied Catholic, 131;
   Captive Bishops, 136; Priests "in
   Search," 138; GFU and GFO,
   142; Midnight Mass with Slides,
   145; The Communion Chants,
   146; St. Marcel I, 147; Plain
   Chant, 149; The Sense of the
   Sacred Has Been Lost, 150; Latin,
   151; "The Mass Has to Be
   Destroyed," 154; God Is God,
   156

7. PROVIDENCE AND THE SEMINARY
      AT ECONE   159
   The First Years, 161; How Econe
   Came into Being, 163; The
   Chauffeurs of the Bishop, 166

8. THE SAVAGE CONDEMNATION   173
   The Apostolic Visitors, 175; The
   Declaration of November 21,
   1974, 177; The Accusation, 180;
   Without Any Form of Process,
   184; Vatican II and the Council of
   Nicea, 187; Sanctions? Null and
   Void, 189

9. "I AM NOT WORRIED"   193
   "I Shall Not Willingly Help the
   Destroyers of the Church," 195;
   The Sufferings of Paul VI, 197;
   Most Holy Father, Accept the
   Experience of Tradition, 198; Paul
   VI's Rage, 201; Cardinal Villot,
   203; Is Liberalism a Sin? 205; St.
   Thomas Aquinas, 209; The
   Seminary of Econe Is Not a
   Command Post, 211

Foreword

The present work is a book of conversations. The initiative was taken by José Hanu, who wanted to serve as the voice of many Catholics concerned about the crisis in the Church.

Since he asked my agreement, I did not think I should refuse. After all, do I not have to profit from any occasion to preach the truth?

Like any other literary form, that of conversations has its limitations and its drawbacks. The questions cannot help but influence the answers, since they have to set up the framework for them. Besides, the one who asks them is led to choose one particular fact over another, not because it is more important, not even because it is closer to the truth, but because it fits the general direction of the conversation better than another.

In this book, the over-all direction was dictated by José Hanu. Had I wanted to talk about my life myself, I would probably not have cited the same facts, nor insisted upon the same points. But, within this limit, I am nevertheless assuming all the responsibility for my replies. I hope that in this way I might contribute to the establishment of the social kingdom of Our Lord Jesus Christ, which is my only aim.

On the Feast of the Immaculate Conception
Econe, December 8, 1976

Marcel Lefebvre

1

"We Are Not Rebels"

AT ECONE

José Hanu: Well, here we are, your Excellency, in the seminary of Ecône which has been the subject of so much talk. Let me first have a good look around.

How lovely and peaceful it is with its modern but modest buildings and the great stone house which once was the property of the Canons of the Great St. Bernard! It seems to be exactly right for its purpose. Besides, it is surrounded by symbols. The snow-capped Alps so close by shout out their purity and strength and the vineyards all around, planted by the monks and cultivated in the same way and always yielding a fine crop, show how effective thousand-year-old rules are.

The high-power lines which extend above the vines in no way bother them, as if to demonstrate that there is no incompatibility between adherence to the past and the demands of modern life.

I take a look at your seminarians, Excellency. They are a fine group of handsome, well-adjusted young men. Their eyes show no trace of disappointment, no anxiety, no fanaticism. They seem so much at ease within themselves and they are wearing the cassock with a kind of natural nobility.

In short, these young men look happy.

I take a look at you, yourself, Excellency, and I am really astonished. You are a seventy-one-year-old bishop who all his life was loyal to the Pope and the Vatican—and whom the Pope and the Vatican have severely punished in the full glare of publicity. You should be prostrate or in revolt. You are, however, serene. Even better than that, you are the embodiment of calm certainty, so rare in these hectic times.

When I look at your seminary, which has been called "wild," and when I see your seminarians whom your opponents have called "visionaries," I tell myself that there must be a tragic error somewhere, that the hullabaloo about your case has prevented Catholics from understanding the essentials, especially the essence of what you, yourself, Excellency, are. This will be the topic of our conversation.

First of all, let me say that my heart is heavy when I think of all those "progressive" Catholics, our brethren, who have slandered you; of the bishops who have mistaken the wind of a politico-religious mood, which too often is destructive, for the breath of the Holy Spirit; and of the Pope himself to whom the wind of this mood undoubtedly has brought incomplete information, either false or distorted.

But the noise of the mass media, their multitude of words, their rash judgments have hidden the core of the questions raised by your actions. These questions are serious and troubling for every Catholic who is attached to the Church.

My heart is heavy when I think of the possible consequences, for a bishop is, after all, also a man with his faults and foibles.

The tug of war between you and the Vatican, after your surprising audience with the Pope, has left an impression of uneasiness.

Then too, your homily at Lille has upset and shaken

me. Your detractors were able to start a whole folklore about you and it came off reeking as triumphalism. It allowed certain people to exclaim: "He has finally dropped the mask: this is an archbishop of the extreme right!"

The trouble is that the right—and that includes the racist right—is trying to claim you; you have only to read the newspapers to be enlightened on this count! Now, as much as I deplore and distrust the faithful and the priests who read the gospel according to Marx, I also fear and reproach those who justify their ideas by pointing to the Cross.

I assume that your language has not expressed your convictions accurately and your enemies, as well as those who are "claiming" you, have lost no time in altering your thought even more.

Have you been, at this critical hour, the victim of Satan's trap? Or was it the Holy Spirit himself who pushed you too far, in order to prove to everybody that a man of the Church—no matter what his origins, his opinions, or his rank—should purge from his vocabulary political considerations which could drive a wedge between him and his brethren? I must admit that this latter explanation would not displease me at all. But I want to state it once and for all: regrettable or not, your sermon at Lille raised a question of capital importance—that of the role of religion in society.

It will be with these matters that our dialogue will concern itself. Some of my questions may well seem sacrilegious to you.

Archbishop Marcel Lefebvre: Sacrilege? No question is

sacrilegious, unless it implies statements which hurt God!

But don't expect too many shades of meaning on my part. I come from the North, where Flemish blood pulses through the veins of most of the inhabitants and the Flemish, as you well know, are famous for their bluntness. It would be difficult to say as much about the Italians and herein perhaps lie the reasons for some of my difficulties with the Vatican.

I refuse to admit, however, that a cause such as that of Our Lord Jesus Christ can be subject to the ups and downs of human thought.

What Often Is Missing Is Courage

We are beginning our dialogue on Christmas Eve, the feast which is the most hopeful feast of the entire year.

Therefore I wish with all my heart that the coming year will finally bring the solution to the crisis which has shaken the Church and which has caused us such painful problems. Our young priests will then be able to exercise their apostolate with the blessings and encouragement which are their due.

Those young priests are anything but rebels, as some people pretend, even at the risk of misusing the word.

How can one call "rebels" those who follow the rules which have been forged by centuries? And how can one call "faithful" those who find it right to reject those rules and even the laws, or who tolerate—

through weakness, if not by demagoguery—such shameful dismantling?

Or how can one designate as "faithful" those who refer respectfully to the Council but come to doubt the divinity of Christ, arguing the point even before the cameras of national television? And "rebels" those who, grounded in their faith, think that the Council Fathers, in their eagerness for an "opening to the world," have edited the texts which, with their imprecision, have opened the door to all sorts of fantasies, to put it kindly?

This was certainly not the intention of the bishops who were assembled at the Council, but the facts speak for themselves. I could quote them by the thousands and I am going to quote you a few right away, if you want me to.

In any case, believe me that I can well understand that Catholics of good faith could let themselves be carried away by baneful ideas and that they fight me—they who constantly use the word "love." Indeed, if one measures the formidable pressures of the modern world, the hostility aimed at me seems natural and even logical.

Unfortunately, what has been lacking, what is always lacking, is firmness, courage, self-denial by those whose mission it is to be firm as rocks, whatever the price.

Consider the dismay of seminarians, for example, whose director of conscience, after having urged over many long years the supreme sacrifice of celibacy, reneges on his vows and marries a divorcee in the nearby chapel. After letting such an "accident" pass without an indignant outcry, can any bishop dare reproach a Catholic couple for breaking the marriage vow?

Still, I can understand the priests who immerse themselves in the world, and the couple whose home life shifts grounds. What I really fail to comprehend is the pretense of judging us, a right which those responsible for such delinquency claim for themselves. Maybe in their heart of hearts they are ashamed of this false example of fidelity? Is it that they hope their conscience will be quieted when such an example is "justified"?

I AM NOT THE HEAD OF THE TRADITIONALISTS

I shall make mine the famous motto: "I shall endure." And I say aloud what Catholics who may have been brainwashed, but whose heart is in the right place, feel in the depth of their souls.

So—don't be mistaken: I am not, I never want to be, I never shall be "the head of the traditionalists," as they want people to believe. As if I would enlist troops to attack the Vatican! This is ridiculous!

I have never "corralled" anybody. It happened simply that the day when I regretted that true vocations might not be able to find true seminaries, vocations presented themselves and many of the faithful and various priests gave us help.

Other faithful and other priests, sometimes huddled together in small places, have asked me to come and comfort them in their despair. Should I refuse to support them in their Catholic faith?

In addition, the suspension clamped on me has provided a publicity which I certainly have not desired.

It has alerted unhappy Catholics all over the world who before did not even know of my existence. They, in turn, are calling me. Whenever I can, I accept their invitation. But I do not direct them at all, I don't regroup them, and even less do I arm them against the Vatican: I simply recommend that they keep the faith in Our Lord Jesus Christ, in the Holy Spirit, and in the Virgin Mary, who—as I hope with all my heart—will make it possible for me to continue my mission within the bosom of the Church.

Therefore, I am not the head of a rebellion. I am only trying to be the shepherd who tries to tend a disoriented flock in the spirit of the first pastor and those who followed him.

This shepherd is now ready to answer your questions.

When I read articles in the press both of the left and of the right, or when I listen to the commentators on the radio, I often ask myself if I am dreaming, or if they talk in Chinese—for it is Greek to me. Well, as Beaumarchais said: "Slander, slander! Something can always be found to slander!" That is why slander is one of the best weapons in Satan's arsenal. About his existence I have no doubt—as you may have guessed, I take it?

Nor has there ever been any doubt about Satan's existence by His Holiness, Paul VI, who on February 29, 1972, declared:

"We have the impression that through some cracks in the wall the smoke of Satan has entered the temple of God: It is doubt, uncertainty, questioning, dissatisfaction, confrontation."

Son of an Industrialist of Tourcoing

A Superficial, Even a False, Image

J.H.: Some of your enemies continue to repeat that you are the son of a textile industrialist from Tourcoing.

M.L.: I could have been the son of a farmer, a lawyer, a miner, a deep-sea fisherman, etc. Do I owe my parents to accident, as you might term it, or to Providence, as I prefer to see it? In any case, these are the facts: I belong to an industrial family from the North. Is this a taint?

J.H.: A socio-political taint! Many "progressive" Catholics who believe that the family environment conditions the individual seem to think so anyhow. I have even heard one of them say that, given your origins, you are "congenitally and therefore irreparably reactionary." In short, unredeemable. To buttress his case, the man brandished all sorts of cliches which contain some truth and which you know so well.

The industrialists from the region of Lille, Roubaix and Tourcoing built their fortune on the labor of twelve-year-old children who have to work in their factories barechested and barefooted in the stifling and humid atmosphere of the textile mills.

Those industrialists take out insurance against Hell by obliging their workmen to arrive five minutes early for work so that they can recite a "Hail Mary" and protect themselves against revolutionary atheism by regularly exacting what they call "letters of confession" from their workers, which are proof that they are being taken in hand by a clergy devoted to capitalism.

Those are the industrialists who had children by the dozen, and whose wealth, amassed from the toil of poor people, was so great that they could give a "chimney"—that is, a plant, to every one of their sons, and a "brick," that is, a million francs, to each of their daughters.

M.L.: Let's be serious! Somewhere in the past, this picture may have had the semblance of truth. But to be rightly understood, it has to be put into historical context and completed. Even if some of the industrialists from Lille-Roubaix-Tourcoing have behaved in this manner, many others had displayed remarkable social concern. There are many witnesses to this.

Besides, the profession of woolweaver, as my father's was, has always been hazardous because it is closely related to the fluctuations of the market. And how many men, some of them most competent and most prudent, have not fallen by the wayside in this venture?

I know what I am talking about because my own father found that he was ruined in 1929, the year of my ordination. My young brothers still remember how our parents tried to protect from seizure their furniture and other family possessions.

During those trying times, my father and mother behaved admirably.

I take great pride also in insisting that they led exemplary lives in every way, especially religious, civic and social. They could not have been like that, if their ideas had not been diametrically opposed to what you have just described.

J.H.: It is true, Excellency, your parents were quite unusual Catholics. That is why I wanted to learn their views before I questioned you. From many points of view, theirs were saintly lives.

I am not going to ask you to tell me about yourself. On the one hand, family modesty will prevent you from telling everything and on the other hand, one might believe that your love for your father and mother might transfigure them.

However, because I think that character or action or a vocation are determined to a certain extent by the family environment, I find it necessary to speak of your parents. I shall therefore tell you what I learned. Please correct me, if my information is wrong.

FAITH AND PATRIOTISM

It was easy for me to learn the memory your parents left with their fellow citizens, for they were typical of certain Catholic couples of the past (I am a child of such myself), for whom the idea of duty dominated everything: religious duty, patriotic duty, duty toward the state, duty toward the family. And it must be stated here that this sense of duty was common to Northern families, workers and middle class alike.

Naturally, the lives of your father and mother were tied together inseparably, but for greater clarity I shall recall them separately.

I can easily picture your father. I am not at all surprised to hear that he, the head of an enterprise, got up early in the morning to attend the six o'clock Mass, receive Holy Communion and recite a decade of the rosary, and went to work ahead of any of his employees: he was far from being the only one to behave like that.

It was normal, too, that he should be the last to leave the workshop and the office and that he would lead the evening family prayer, kneeling before a crucifix, just before the younger children were sent to bed. There was no scarcity of small children: your father gave your mother eight of them. With many other Catholic families in the North in those days, they considered a large family a gift from God.

To your father's religious profile, already quite pronounced I should say, two other traits must be added.

At age eighteen, your father had joined the stretcher-bearers of Notre Dame de Lourdes, and never abandoned this helpful mission. He also joined the Third Order of St. Francis, and thus wore a scapular to recall the hard rules of that order which he had vowed to follow in part. He wanted to be "one of the best Children of Mary" and he certainly imposed great sacrifices upon himself "to merit Heaven." Today this seems like a dream, but it was a fact. I have to repeat, furthermore, that the case of your father was not an isolated one.

When World War I broke out in 1914, he was only thirty-five years old but he already had six children, which brought him exemption from front-line duty. He should have been glad about it but, instead, he felt ashamed.

After the first battle in nearby Belgium, he joined a society for injured war veterans. At the wheel of his own automobile, he crossed the French and German lines several times to collect, under fire, the most seriously wounded French and Allied soldiers and to transport them to the military hospital at Tourcoing.

After the Germans occupied Tourcoing, he organized the evacuation of English prisoners and helped the Belgian secret service. Finally, in January of 1915, when he heard that his exhausted country was mobilizing new recruits, he went to Paris, hoping that he could enlist in the regiment in which he had served once before. It was in vain: in the eyes of the recruiters six children were reason enough to stay out of battle.

Since he spoke English and German fluently (as, by the way, most of the Northern industrialists did), he presented himself to the secret service. For the rest of the war, he was one of their most active liaison agents for the Intelligence branch. He had taken the name of Lefort, constantly scurrying between England and France, Belgium and Holland, and, of course, constantly in danger of his life.

Such a valiant man was not going to give in when, eleven years later, misfortune struck. He repeated with Job: "God has given me everything, God has taken everything, praised be the name of God," but he also professed: "Help yourself and God will help you." He succeeded in reestablishing himself, with "the help of Providence," as he used to say regularly.

At the end of the second war there was another occupation. He was sixty-two years old, but where would he be found? In the service of France, of course.

But his patriotism proved to be fatal for him. The Germans, who had put him under surveillance, distrusted him more than anyone else: arrest, trial and deportation to Sonnenburg followed, and finally death. His comrades in captivity reported his extraordinary courage in the midst of indescribable privations, under the fists of his jailers and, even, of his male nurses, in a repugnant cell. They told, above all, how his unshakeable faith was of immense help to all those around him.

Sometimes your father was allowed to write from prison to his family. Your family was good enough to let me see the text of a letter he wrote on September 9, 1941. This document in some way constitutes his testament. Here are the most moving passages:

"I am awaiting the hour of Providence. What is certain is that here we are gaining some small merits and getting a good foretaste of Purgatory. I am sorry for those who are in my circumstances but lack the comfort of religion.

"There were terrible moments, but I have felt God's help. I could see that I was helped in the moments when I felt the lowest. For all this, I thank God. Suffering purifies.

"It will be a great sacrifice not to be able to see my children before I die. I bless them with all my heart and confide them to Our Lady, the Virgin Mary, who was so good to me. She loves my family, who will always remain consecrated to her and who will always seek through her the extension of the reign of her Divine Son."

The life of your father, Excellency, was thus an

exemplary one for a Christian and a patriot. I cannot help thinking that his example had far-reaching effects on you. For there are many similarities between you and this scrupulous and ardent Catholic, that fighter, that Resistance man who never gave in to the enemy, not even when the enemy seemed to triumph—that obstinate man who accepted adversity without bowing his head.

Knowing your devotion to the Virgin Mary and to what you mystically seem to call the reign of Christ, one has the impression that this last message still lives in you as vibrant and as clear as when you received it thirty-five years ago.

SEVERITY AND MORAL STRICTNESS

However, as the members of your family have confided to me without prodding, the extreme moral strictness of your father was often very difficult for the young people. His severity may have been excessive.

M.L.: Why talk about strictness and severity? We should rather call it "austerity." But an austerity which was mellowed and—oh, how much—refined by a perfect family life! It was a perfect union which the family members still remember—all the brothers and sisters who are still living—across the abyss of fifty years!

J.H.: That severity of your father, it is true, did not lead the children to rebellion, nor to a nervous breakdown, nor to vice.

M.L.: Look at this family photo: Five of the children became priests or nuns, all happy in their lives consecrated to God, whereas a "modern" psychiatrist, looking at a person of such background and education, would probably have sworn that they all left the house, slamming the door behind them, to embrace drugs and prostitution!

As for the others, established in the world, you have been able to assume yourself that they are not alienated.

When we were young, all Catholic children were educated in the same manner, whereas, today, families who still have the courage to have their offspring so educated find themselves pitched into a climate so permissive that it often undermines their efforts or even nullifies them.

It can therefore happen that the son of a Catholic who is "rigid" finds himself encouraged by his friends, or by a teacher in high school, or by modern Catholic literature, to revolt, and that this revolt leads him to the worst degradation. But the environment, not the parent, is to blame for this.

On purpose, I referred to certain high school teachers and modern Catholic literature, for the spectacle of our times is that the teaching clergy, whose mission is to put backbone into characters and souls, have permitted themselves to be led astray or have even gone halfway to perversion. Today, "authority" is always wrong, especially when vested in a person. And the atmosphere, since we are, above all, people steeped in Christianity, is gravely affected by this situation.

You will now understand why I bless the "rigorism"—the severity of the home where I first saw the light of the world.

I Shall Die a Monarchist

J.H.: But your father was a dyed-in-the-wool monarchist, wasn't he? The letter I cited does not make any bones about it:

"Be of good courage and patience, for the situation will clear up and we shall have good days for Our Dear Country, returned to its beautiful traditions, which the disorder will have reduced to ruin.

"You know that I am dying a Catholic, a Frenchman and a monarchist. For I think that it is only with the establishment of Christian monarchies that Europe and the world can retain their stability and true peace."

Maybe it is here, in the piety of the son or in the piety of the family, that one could find an explanation of some of the passages of your sermon at Lille which has astonished so many people?

I have an exact transcript of that sermon. May I quote some excerpts?

"By now the theses and the principles of liberal Catholicism are officially accepted. And what did the liberal Catholics desire for the last century and a half, if not the marriage of the Church to the Revolution? This is the reason why, for a century and a half, the Supreme Pontiffs have condemned liberal Catholicism: they have refused to bless the marriage with those who worship Reason, who sent priests to the scaffold and persecuted nuns. Remember the prison ships of Nantes, where the faithful priests were crammed together to send them to the bottom!

"Now this is what the Revolution did. But let me tell you, my dear brethren, what the Revolution did was nothing compared to what Vatican II did by espousing liberalism. It would have been much better if the 40,000 or 50,000 priests who abandoned the cassock all over the world, who have gone back on their vows before God, would have died as martyrs, had gone to the gallows. At least they would have gained their souls! Now they risk losing them.

"The union of Church and Revolution is adulterous. And from such an adulterous union, nothing but bastards can come forth. And who or what are the bastards? Our rites. The rite of the Mass is a bastard rite! . . ."

I have to admit that your choice of words—"bastard"—seemed bold to me, but it also struck me as very well chosen. It gives me a certain exhilaration.

But there is this spectre of liberalism. M. Giscard d'Estaing speaks of "advanced liberalism," that spectre, above all, of the Revolution. Are you too a royalist? A belated royalist? Because the Revolution has done a lot of damage, but it has permitted the breakup of feudalism, and feudalism, especially in the social field, had few elements that were Christian.

M.L.: Yes, my father was a monarchist but I do not think that this constitutes a blemish. As far as I am concerned, I have never lent my name to any kind of political party whatever. Besides, the example of so many monarchs who betrayed their mission, as have so many bishops, certainly does not encourage one to be a monarchist!

In the meantime this is the fact and we cannot deny it: the Church *is* a monarchy.

As far as my sermon at Lille is concerned, it was an echo of what all the Sovereign Pontiffs have always alleged, and that which they always have condemned, except since Vatican II. That's why the sermon was Catholic, not political.

There were certainly abuses to be reformed in 1889, but there is a wide abyss between those reforms and destroying religion itself and, furthermore, tearing down kings because they upheld religion.

The last Council has acted in nearly the same fashion, but in order to put through some useful reforms it has gone in search of the leading principles of liberalism. And these principles, logically enough, have given the deathblow to the Church.

To get back to my father, do you think he asked, while he was risking his life in 1914 to save the wounded, "Are you a royalist?" And that he abandoned those who were not? Many of the people who testified with great emotion to the physical and moral help he gave them in the German Sonnenburg Prison held political opinions which were diametrically opposed to his.

Besides, there is one fact which is of special significance for his social ideas: In 1920 he entered the city council of Tourcoing, where he remained to the day of his arrest in 1941. Would one have had confidence in him for so many years, especially during the major social trouble which marked that period, if he were not a just man and profoundly human? In fact—and all opinions tend to agree on this point—he was a moderate and tender man. Considering himself a brother in Jesus Christ to his fellowmen, he thought that he had to set an example to his brethren, whatever the cost. This is undoubtedly the most beautiful lesson he could give me and I shall remember it to my dying days in my heart and in my spirit.

J.H.: Here is an interesting question: Did your father conform at the time of the Vatican's censure of Action Française?

M.L.: Look how history is written! My father had monarchist convictions but he was far too levelheaded to get involved in the Action Française! What a pity for my enemies!

BENEDICTIONS AND GRACES

J.H.: Now I want to recall the astonishing personality of your mother, who was born Gabrielle Watin and, in the opinion of all who knew her, was a saint.

I have a small book which was meant for her children, grandchildren and great-grandchildren, so that her example would serve for their edification. This booklet was edited by a priest in 1941, which probably explains the cloying style. With your permission, I want to give you an example of that style, not as a mockery, but to show how certain great families of the North were "steeped in piety."

"Gabrielle's father was a wise man, just and good. He dedicated himself completely to his duty to the state. Small wonder, then, that in his stable and special household God should have brought forth a chosen soul. Three cradles had preceded hers and three were to follow. Providence had thus placed her between her brothers and sisters to become their source of joy. She grew and unfolded like a flower in the atmosphere of the family. When she was still quite young, one could characterize her as a daughter to duty.

"The education she received strengthened this effort. Her mother, before joining her husband to attend the seven o'clock Mass every morning, made the round of the children's rooms to offer the day to God. Before the noon and the evening meal, grace and benediction were said together. At the end of the day, a prayer was recited together."

M.L.: I don't doubt that the writing stems from another epoch and that one would write differently today. But he is quite right in describing the atmosphere in which my mother grew up.

Now, and at greater length, because we have to develop some facts, I want to talk a little about the benediction and the graces which were said in my mother's family, as they were said in all Catholic families, though today they are forgotten or derided.

Benediction and grace are the testimony of the gratefulness of human beings who hold themselves accountable for the fruits of this earth, given to them by God. If families today would take the trouble to recite them, they would be more conscious of the scandalous mess of our consumer society.

Since we are speaking of my mother, I want to say that when she was rich, when one did not care about a piece of bread thrown away, she taught us not to throw away anything, not to spoil anything, even if it were only a pin.

I only hope that my seminarians at Econe, who also are reciting this benediction and grace, will be filled with the same spirit.

A WOMAN OF EXCEPTIONAL CHARACTER

J.H.: Your mother, Excellency, was of exceptional character. I would like to say that she was a woman of character.

She proved it especially during 1914-1918. For four years, with her husband at war and six children at home, she fulfilled several tasks: she managed the factory, cared for the wounded, visited the sick, the old and poor, and withstood the demands of the German occupation, which led to her being sent to jail in a dank and unheated cell, where her only food consisted of tainted gruel.

The head of the German *Kommandatur*, probably a "correct Prussian," was greatly annoyed at the treatment meted out by his police to this lady of distinction. He went to see her in person, promising to set her free if she would write a letter asking for pardon. She was cold, she was hungry, she was terribly worried about her children, but she refused.

When she finally became gravely ill, friends had to implore her before at last she consented to write a word. But she was careful not to promise anything nor to ask for pardon; she simply wrote, "I admit that I was in the wrong in the eyes of the German authority." The head of the *Kommandatur* was furious but he had to let her go. She went with her head held high.

How is it possible for us, Excellency, hearing of your mother's comportment in this episode, not to compare it with your own obstinate attitude in your conflict with the Vatican?

She proved to be a woman of character during the time of your father's financial difficulties. She was at his side everywhere, replacing employees whom he had to lay off. She took over the functions of the comptroller. The personnel revered her for her courage, her humanity, and some of them went so far as to indicate that salvaging the enterprise was due entirely to her actions.

But, Excellency, forgive me this question which will shock your piety as a son: Was the marriage of your parents a happy one? It is true that the pious pen which retraced the life of your mother points out in every line that your parents founded an exemplary household. But she also dropped remarks like this:

"Even if there were some misunderstandings in the intimacy of the house, mutual and profound love and a great Christian spirit always protected the union of the hearts."

One could add here what your mother herself confided: "What does it matter if the passengers get hurt by some tangle of oars? Is it not a sign that they advance? And what happiness will there be when, once the other bank is reached, they will find themselves together in peace?"

And finally the remark of one of your sisters, a nun: "In this marriage God had encapsulated two choice jewels, very different, one from the other, who were called to fashion each other."

M.L.: Far from shocking my filial piety, the evidence makes it even stronger!

Man and woman of character, my parents at a young age had to face up to their temperaments. Had they lived in our age, without ideals and without illusions, their union might have undergone painful trials. But they prayed to God together and he gave them the patience, humility and the gift of openness with each other which permitted them to realize how profound their mutual love was, and how their personal concepts could harmonize and complement each other.

In fact, theirs was an exemplary marriage and they gave to all Christians around them a wonderful example—that kind of example that the priests of today should impart to young couples to strengthen their marriage, rather than show that they understand the reasons for division, which only aggravates the motives and invariably leads so many priests to admit the scandal of divorce.

What a disaster for the home and above all for the children!

DEATH OF A SAINT

J.H.: But your mother was not only a woman of

character, the wife who, by a union of spirit, came to adopt her husband's political views (when she was a good republican); she also led a very ardent religious life. We have to remember that she came from a family of the North whose Christian convictions made colossal human contributions. Her great-grandfather, who died in 1810, had 1200 descendants by 1940, of whom there were more than sixty priests, religious and nuns.

In this family, as your mother's book describes, there was no mollycoddling in education: only virile Christian education. Could we have been there on a typical evening, we would have seen the youngsters on their knees, their arms crossed before them, reciting their prayers by heart, and the parents in the background, checking on their fervor and devotion. You were never a half-hearted Christian.

Small wonder that your mother, heir to such a Christian tradition, veered toward mysticism. Those close to her state that, during the long years of suffering, which were supported with a "heavenly smile," she really died the death of a saint. Some of her descendants say that they never prayed to her in vain, that she always interceded in their favor.

You, Excellency, who certainly often pray to her—do you believe that she is helping you from above? Do you think she agrees with you, that she does not regret your breach with the Vatican—or maybe she is asking you not to give in?

M.L.: My answer comes both from the heart and the mind. To every human being who had the fortune of being brought up as I was, such a mother appears to be a saint.

I did not try to find out about the mystic ways of my mother, because she was so modest and humble that she never talked about them to me. They were the inviolable secrets of her soul. It was sufficient for me to have experienced her maternal tenderness, which was inexhaustible.

But if we have to wait for our beloved deceased to guide us, where are our own merits? Is it not the example which they have given us, while living here with us, which we, those living today, should force ourselves to follow in our way, steadfast in our faith and our vocation?

Yes, I pray to her. Often. Yes, I ask that my mother and father, united in eternal happiness, help me to be as strong as they were.

I believe that my father and mother look down on me. But my self-presumption, if I pretended to quote a much-used modern expression, to be "in tune with them," would be unacceptable to them.

Out of modesty and discretion, I leave it to others to speak of the extraordinary graces that have come to them through the intercession of my mother. In truth, I should not be much surprised. Hers was a privileged soul.

But it is necessary to maintain a careful, even suspicious attitude when it comes to supernatural interventions, for it is often distressing to know the spirit that is behind such messages. I prefer to keep to my faith as it was taught me by my dear parents, by their steadfast words and, above all, by their example. I ask them to let me be unshakeable in this Catholic faith, as they themselves were.

Action Française Questioned

A Child without Problems

J.H.: The conversation about your parents, your Excellency, makes me think of the vivid remarks of one of your enemies—and not the least of them—who during a public debate reproached a traditional Catholic for having recalled their example: "As if the parents of Archbishop Lefebvre were of any importance! You have been dazzled by priestly flimflam. You are starting to tell us the life of a new St. Marcel just when that Marcel has cut himself off from the Church! That is a sin against the Holy Spirit!"

It is true that every Catholic today thinks the Holy Spirit is on his side, as if he were the spirit of contradiction.

Some of your friends would have preferred to see you come from quite a different background. For example, if you had been the son of a modern dancer, what mortification it would have been for the "integrists," a little too much inclined to respect virtue only when it is hereditary. They might even have snubbed you and, luckily, this would have deprived you of some very embarrassing friends.

But often, while I was in revolt myself—and this despite a family much like yours—I would have wished to see you as the end product of a difficult childhood, hear you tell about your flight from home at age sixteen, your bouts with psychiatrists who were anxious to see in the rebellion of an adolescent the future bishop's break with the "conciliar Church."

But since my task here is to analyze and criticize you just as you are, I have to admit: the troubles and the thoughtless actions which are so much part of growing up never bothered you. Search as I might among those who have known you before Vatican II, I have found nobody who could have said that, even once in your life before that Council, you had questioned the authority of your superiors.

"Marcel," said your brothers and sisters, "was a child with absolutely no problems whatsoever. He worked admirably and without difficulty; he had an even disposition."

But maybe you were an obstinate child? Many who were at Vatican II repeatedly say: "Obstinate? Oh, yes—he is obstinate as a mule."

But your family thinks otherwise. They say you were an eager and contented child. Whenever you had made a decision, you stuck to it without relaxing, until you had accomplished as much as you could under the circumstances.

Your family also expresses admiration for your many talents, such as your manual dexterity and your sense of organization. They remember how, when you were a seminarian, you had got the notion to install electricity, at least on the first floor of your father's house, and that "he did it all by himself, with the skill and the competence of a professional." It seems that, on vacation, you rose before everybody else, set the breakfast table to save work for your mother, and did it "without forgetting anything, with care and a certain artistic flair."

I am told that before furnishing your seminary at

Econe, you went to all the merchants in Fribourg to choose, by yourself, all the china, silver, tablecloths, drapes, etc. You did it "with the competence of a knowledgeable housewife."

M.L.: At the beginning we were only a few. We were poor and we had to economize. But it is also true that I think the setting or environment should not be neglected. Harmony in the material order fosters harmony in the soul.

But now, before giving credence to all the good things said about me, I want you to understand my family's preoccupation.

Because of their upbringing, tradition and personal convictions, this family adheres strictly to the unity of the Church. My difficulties with the Vatican, which cause more or less friendly discussion among them, trouble them more than they would let people believe. Some of them certainly have doubts on my account, even if they love me very much. Therefore, they band together to point out that Marcel was a good child, an exemplary young man, and—beween the lines—this means that I would have to have very serious reasons.

Yes, I do have serious reasons, but that does not mean that my childhood was that of an angel!

J.H.: Your family gets a kick out of reading that the Vatican hierarchy finds you not only obstinate but also "not subtle." This, if true, would lead to some irritating questions, such as: If they themselves, the Vatican hierarchy, are so intelligent, how is it they promoted you first to bishop, then to archbishop and finally to apostolic delegate for all of Africa?

Your sharp sense of humor, as your brothers say, nourished by the good sense for which the people of Tourcoing are known, has probably prompted you to ask that question yourself.

The terms in which you commented about the suspension declared by your "good friends and benefactors" were not without relish. You wrote them:

"I have been deprived of my right to celebrate Mass, to consecrate the host, to preach in consecrated places, which means that I have been forbidden to celebrate the new Mass, to confer the new sacraments and to preach the new doctrine.

"Therefore, since I reject precisely these novelties, I have in this way been officially enjoined from using them. As it is, I am deprived of something which I do not desire!"

You immediately seized on the ridiculous aspects of a tragic situation. I consider this ability to dramatize as a great gift.

Anyhow, your entourage has told me the conditions under which you learned about your "punishment."

You were at home with your family. Shortly before noon a messenger delivered a message of obvious importance. You left it unopened on the table where it had been put and took part in the family's noon meal with a gusto which did not seem artificial. Then you picked up your letter and went up to your room, not to come down again until the evening meal. And again, you were an articulate dinner guest.

M.L.: Yes, surely, I did expect a sort of suspension, but to tell you the truth I had hoped that it would never come. I was thinking more of my family and friends, who would be more affected by it than myself. I am convinced that the fruits of injustice will be reaped by those who meted them out in the first place. All one has to do is wait.

IN GOLD LETTERS

As you said, I waited for the end of the lunch before I opened the letter, which announced my censure. Why did I do this? In observance of an old proverb, "There is a time for everything," a proverb which our Catholic religion makes a kind of duty, so often forgotten in our days but, alas, so right.

Had I opened that letter immediately, I would have upset the family and spoiled their meal, for it would have been very difficult for me to hide my emotions. I might have shown a moment of weakness, or bitterness which does not become a priest, especially not a bishop, even if one is on familiar terms with him.

Finally, I want to say a word about the attraction which manual labor has for me and on this occasion honor an old custom of the industrialists of Tourcoing, even though those heads of factories are disparaged today.

As you might know—but, in general, it is not known in France—those factory owners liked to send their sons out into the workshops when they were quite young, to work side by side with the workmen. Of course, as one has pointed out quite often, this apprenticeship was often at the detriment of intellectual development. At any rate, all those sons of rich families were able to use all ten of their fingers.

It might be that I owe my taste for puttering around, which I share with many sons of factory owners of my generation in Tourcoing, to this custom of making manual dexterity something of value for the middle class. Unfortunately, I do not have the time for such activity, but I always think that, since God has given us a body and a soul, one has to do something to maintain an equilibrium between the two. When one is, for instance, cutting wood (and I love to split wood), one cannot look right or left but has to concentrate on cutting with the grain.

Now I am convinced that many false notions stem from brains that are cut off from reality and live in the unreal atmosphere of myths.

In his time, the good Pope Piux X had to face similar errors. But since he had both feet planted in reality, he was able to stand up against them.

THE FRENCH SEMINARY
IN ROME

J.H.: I shall not ask you about your days at the seminary at Tourcoing. You were a good pupil. You were not like a genius who loses his crown on the day of the prizes because he stumbles under the weight of books, nor like a dunce who gets a consolation prize. In short, you were a student who does not leave many memories, because he has always worked regularly. Your enemies in the North enjoy thinking of you as a very average boy.

I have asked them how they could explain that this

boy could one day become the archbishop of Dakar and then the founder of a seminary in Switzerland, against all sorts of opposition, finally to become the conscience which is shaking the whole Church. They remained nonplussed about that and it seems that the idea never entered their heads that this transformation might be the work of the Holy Spirit.

One might also think that He was busy with you because you had a vocation, a simple vocation, I might say, which developed along its own lines.

At the end of your philosophy year, you joined the French Seminary in Rome, which, according to your opponents, was "a refuge for aristocrats."

M.L.: That's what they also like to say about Econe. This is absolutely ridiculous and untrue.

J.H.: Nevertheless, I checked into the origins of the young men who came from the diocese of Lille and studied at the French Seminary in Rome at the time you were there.

It is true that they all were, if not aristocrats, sons of industrialists, rich merchants, etc., in short, of the upper middle classes. But the fault for this lies in the diocese itself. While all other dioceses awarded their scholarships to poor people with good minds, Lille did nothing of the sort. As a result, only the young men whose families could shoulder the heavy burden of room and board at the French Seminary could pursue their theological and other studies in the Eternal City.

Why Cardinal Lienart, at the time considered by most people as on the extreme left, permitted this is beyond my understanding.

M.L.: It seems to me that Cardinal Lienart did not particularly care for the French Seminary in Rome. In my special case, he wanted me to take my studies in the seminary at Lille. But the wartime conditions had already sent my older brother to the Roman seminary. My parents, therefore, thought it better to send me there too. I have to admit that I was a bit afraid. Wasn't it true that all the courses were given in Latin? I have always had very cordial relations with Cardinal Lienart. Since he consecrated me a bishop and ordained me to the priesthood, I have always regarded him as a sort of spiritual father. Unfortunately, when the Council began, our views began to differ more and more.

J.H.: Well, just as one swallow does not make a summer, so the dozen residents of the seminary from Lille did not make up a patrician clan. Among them were a good many young men of modest circumstances but superior intelligence, the scholarship holders of other dioceses.

But, according to your enemies, it was the manner of recruiting which made the French Seminary one of the most active in Action Française.

Actually, if the ideas of Maurras had found a home there, it was for completely different reasons.

In order to dig further, I interviewed a number of clergy whose careers in the Church were more or less fortunate, all of them former students at Rome with you. Most of them are still very active, their memories excellent and their spirits high. And I tell it as I see it; you yourself seem to be in excellent form.

M.L.: You must not always trust appearances! But I am grateful to God, who still lets me be active in his service.

J.H.: Your colleagues in the seminary in Rome talked to me about the time you were there, that is, under the pontificate of Pius XI. This was also the era in which the "progressives" considered the seminary as "integrist." They detested its rector, Father Le Floch, a Breton, who they suspected was an ardent follower of Maurras.

But Father Le Floch was also a priest who commanded respect. He was adored even by those who fought his opinions. I was told that he was "a humane spirit as well as an impressive character, a man who wielded a great deal of influence, aided by a good sense of humor."

Father Le Floch had played a discreet but important role under Pius X, the preceding Pope. It was rumored that quite a few bishops around the world owed him their mitres and the cardinals' hats. It is difficult to understand, therefore, that some of his seminarians wanted to espouse his ideas under the Action Française label.

But on December 20, 1926, Pius XI condemned Charles Maurras and immediately the "progressives" at the Vatican pulled all sorts of strings to have him sent back to France. When the first apostolic visitor, Cardinal Schuster, found nothing suspect, a second was dispatched and his report was unfavorable.

From that time on, the French Seminary in Rome underwent difficult times. There followed a strict inquiry, the dispatch of Father Le Floch back home, and the dispersal of all seminarians, suspect of adherence to Maurras, to other seminaries. There they had a great deal of leisure to contemplate that they had probably not chosen the path that leads to becoming "a prince of the Church." Now the question comes up, your Excellency: Did you, too, belong to the "scruffy black sheep"—spiritual sons of Charles Maurras?

M.L.: To tie Father Le Floch into the Action Française seems exaggerated to me. I have spent three years under the authority of Father Le Floch and I have never heard him so much as speak of Charles Maurras.

Even if a handful of seminarians were French Actionists, the greater part of them were busy only with their studies and with leading a holy life. Anyhow, that was all I did.

J.H.: This is also what I found out. Six months of canonical inquiry are time enough to develop suspicions, and for denouncers to come to a decision, but not a breath of all this so much as touched you.

Therefore we should believe your colleagues when they say that you were completely disinterested in the Action Française. Even those who at this moment—excuse me for mentioning it—do not hold you "in the odor of sanctity" say: "He was very pious, very exact in the duties of his calling and in the confraternity. He worked a great deal and did not take a stand on anything."

One of them rather condescendingly told me: "He was so modest that I was really surprised when he became bishop of Dakar. I asked myself: How will 'good Marcel' cope?"

You, nevertheless, obtained your doctorate in philosophy while other minds, who do not think themselves inferior, never got so far. It is probable that among themselves they rationalize this by saying: "We? We are not as obstinate as donkeys."

I wonder, then, where your enemies obtained their information, when they wrote that you were a pure product of the Action Française?

I owe the answer not to any of your schoolmates but to a lay person who watched the canonical inquiry from close by. He told me:

"When I learned about the recent declarations of Archbishop Lefebvre and when I read again his Lille sermon, I had an idea: In Rome he played his game very well. He was an unconditionally devoted disciple of Monsignor Le Floch."

This, your Excellency, is how history is written!

M.L.: What hasty and nonsensical judgments!

I, for my part, loved the Roman French Seminary. It taught us to model ourselves according to the magisterium of the Church. It gave us as examples the martyrs who shed their blood for the Catholic faith. I continue to live according to the teachings I received there.

J.H.: I want to talk more about the Roman French Seminary. Your schoolmates whom I interviewed made the astonishing remark: Under Father Le Floch the majority of the seminarians were rather "integrist" inclined. Under his successor, an unconditional Vatican man, the majority were no longer so. This was before the students were sent to other schools.

Do we have to come to the disappointing conclusion that even the intelligent young people, those destined to become the leaven of the Church, are like a flock of sheep?

M.L.: These thoughts surprise me. They do not at all correspond to reality. As a matter of fact, the seminarians who stayed suffered a great deal because of what had happened. One might even say that the French Seminary in Rome has never recovered from those events. Indeed, it has constantly declined.

THE CURATE OF LOMME

J.H.: Your Excellency, we have to talk more about the Action Française, because Father Yves Congar (who is not at all unfavorable toward you) has written in his last book, *Challenge to the Church: The Case of Archbishop Lefebvre* [Our Sunday Visitor, 1977]:

"Everything we have heard about the formation of Archbishop Lefebvre, everything we know about his actions at Dakar, everything that we have heard about him during the Council, points to his being a man on the right, according to the position of the old Action Française."

Father Congar, it seems, owes his information mostly to a book, *Le Drame d' Econe*, recently published by a Swiss priest, Abbe Jean Anzevui, who was often and most cordially received in your seminary.

In cauda venenum (The poison is in the tail); but even

a poisoned source can render praise despite itself. For example:

"His African companions are unanimous in recognizing his 'magnificent missionary past,' his politeness, his openness, his simple natural distinction, his dignity of a perfect life, his austerity, his piety and his total dedication to the task which he set himself. Some of them say that there was in him a 'sweet obstinacy.' "

The aim of the book is to make you out a devil, because it starts with a facsimile of a letter by the abbot of the Great St. Bernard that does not show any signs of originality in its choice of words. The abbot writes:

"I hope this work will serve to scatter the fumes behind which the Evil One hides, in order to fish in troubled waters. . . ."

But this work, full of typical ecclesiastical hypocrisy, now serves as a basic guide even for those who wish to defend you. And by some kind of osmosis, it leads them to use comparable methods.

Abbe Anzevui flatters you by showing how very objective he is—in order to put you down more decisively. The others demolish you at the outset, so that nobody can reproach them for thinking your course of action might have its positive side. Does all this not anger you?

M.L.: In a battle like the one I am conducting at Econe, one has to have trust in God. He will judge. As far as I am concerned, when I am called to the judgment seat I hope to be able to say that, by maintaining the true priesthood, I have not helped to destroy but to build up the Church. Isn't that our main concern?

J.H.: Well, if Father Congar, instead of relying on hearsay, had gone to Lomme, the workmen's quarters at the outskirts of Lille, where you were pastor after your return from the French Seminary in Rome, and if he had interviewed some of the old people there, he would not have heard them speak of the Action Française but of "a young priest of radiant faith." The only anecdote which can still be remembered by the people of that city—and I report it faithfully—is the following:

"An old anticlerical was dying and fiercely refused any spiritual aid. But his family pressured him so much that he finally said: 'I agree, but only on condition that the priest you call is the young pastor: he at least is nobody's toady.' "

I must say that this anecdote is so edifying that your enemies will be suspicious of it, but that's all I found. Besides, I find nothing extraordinary in the fact that the faith of a young priest should overcome the obstacles of a dying anticlerical. Isn't it quite natural?

M.L.: I did only what any priest should do.

THE BISHOP OF DAKAR

J.H.: From Lomme, you joined the Fathers of the Holy Spirit, a missionary congregation. Your older brother, recently deceased, who belonged to the same congregation and who performed his apostolate in Gabon, suggested to you that you should consecrate yourself to the missions in that part of Africa. One would have assumed that "good Marcel" would have stayed with a forlorn mission for life, where his "mediocre intelligence" could have done a lot of good. But after your experiments in that territory, the Fathers of the Holy Spirit catapulted you first to professor, then to superior of the seminary in Gabon, and finally to bishop of Dakar in Senegal. Does one have to believe with your enemies, who have a sharp tongue and very little charity, that the Fathers of the Holy Spirit appointed you in the hope that they would finally get the luminaries of whom they were deprived, although the Third Person does not let himself be so easily trapped?

I can only note here that, hardly installed at Dakar, you, the new archbishop, showed such decision, such organization, such a modern spirit and even avant-garde thinking, that it was absolutely astonishing. You were also very popular among the missionaries, whether they were of the order of the Fathers of the Holy Spirit or not.

You had an extraordinary impact on the diocese. You developed primary schools, reopened secondary schools, extended and coordinated Catholic Action, inspired many vocations among the Senegalese, and increased the number of parishes and missions. When the help from the Fathers of the Holy Spirit was no longer sufficient, your dynamism persuaded priests, brothers and religious from other congregations and orders to come and join you in Senegal.

You gave the missions refrigerators and Jeeps, which they lacked and for which they clamored. Unfortunately, the missionaries in Senegal did not understand that only a bishop of the right, in accord with the position of Action Française, could have obtained these things for them!

Now one can see clearly that refrigerators and Jeeps brought scandal, because they introduced creature comforts for the missionaries which the poor and backward people around them could not enjoy! Even worse, it was a sign of prestige, aimed at impressing these people in order to lead them to conversion! Detestable moral pressure! An attack on liberty!

M.L.: You are right to ridicule all this. At least that's what I do when I read all that nonsense which is being said and written today. Besides, those are all secondary issues.

To be sure, I never made a distinction between European and non-European missionaries. But it is strange to pretend that in every sense the former had to live like the natives. How many died within the first two years of their stay in Africa because they could not even draw nourishment from the local food?

And the Jeeps were used to visit the most distant tribes, to bring them all the benefits of the Gospel, and material and spiritual good works.

If I understand these armchair theoreticians correctly, as Catholic bishop of Dakar I should have used the money—collected in the parishes of France—in an animistic and Moslem country to construct mosques and to offer cars to the witch doctors, instead of giving it to our Catholic missionaries. The delinquency of certain Catholic brains astounds the imagination.

It was you, wasn't it, who told me of the sad fate of two missionaries in the French territories of Afars and Issas who used to drug themselves with *khat*, together with the natives. They put on Moslem gowns and, to top it all, prayed to Allah.

The effect was not at all what they had expected. The Moslems began to look down on them and to take them for inconsistent people. We might dedicate this anecdote to certain bishops who take the charity and respect of the Moslem soul for weakness and compromise.

Make no mistake: I deeply respect the Moslem, much more than those who ignore them; I had the most cordial relationship with them and I accepted a great number of their children in my schools.

But just as some Moslems say about certain Catholics, "You would make a good Moslem," so could we say to many among them that they would make good Catholics. Therefore, I took it to be my duty to try to convert them to Jesus Christ, by my example and by my preaching. Where do you see Action Française in all this?

J.H.: Father Congar reveals his true character as a man of the right in referring to the fact that the archbishop of Dakar was moved to speak of private property, whereas in Africa all property is communal.

M.L.: I know where that comes from: Father Lebret. He asserts that collective property, as in the *kolkhozes*, fits Africans better than private property. This is absurd. In fact, wherever an African acquires a house, or a little piece of land, he works to conserve it; he beautifies it and cultivates fruits. And he is proud to show the fruits of his labor.

In truth, just as slavery was always against human

nature, the sense of property is innate in the human being.

Does Father Congar (whom I never met in the territory) believe that Senegal, proud and independent and mistress of herself, would have rejected private property? Does he think that the city of Dakar, one of the prettiest in Africa, is a communal city, a communal good? You have to understand that when Catholics attempt to rank missionaries' lives in a colonial enterprise, it is because they have never set foot in the country or they were too well received on their visits as tourists.

Were they imperialists or capitalists—the people I found weakened by jaundice, hepatitis, sleeping sickness or marsh fever—who, in spite of this, forced themselves to fulfill their ministry, to bring help to the sick and to convert? Yes, to convert!

Must one believe that, because they had to live and to preach the Gospel, that these missionaries had to spit on their own civilization and on their country, France, the elder daughter of the Church? Does one think that, because they were Christians, they had to preach revolt and revolution? Undoubtedly, they would have found it normal if, in a "fraternal" spirit, they had converted to fetishism!

You can see the result of this new spirit: there are no more missionaries. And the African missions, once so beautiful and flourishing, are trying to make a hodgepodge of all the cults. Is this the new way to the salvation of souls?

You Either Are a Bishop or You Are Not

J.H.: Your enemies allege that at Dakar you established a personality cult. According to them, your photo could be found in most Senegalese houses, "grandly draped in episcopal robes, mitre on your head and a cross in your hands." Please note once more that this allegation rests on rather uncertain testimony. The majority of your enemies were not at Dakar when you were there. I happen to have been all through the Senegal in those days. If I remember having met you in the archdiocese, I cannot remember having seen your picture in the houses of the Senegalese where I was received.

M.L.: Maybe you did not see well, for it happened that families whom I visited or who were received by me, or whose son I baptized or whose daughter I married, felt greatly honored and it made them want to display my photo in their houses, exactly as one displays family photos. Is it not a custom in Catholic households, even in Europe, to display the photo of the bishop of the diocese? At least this was the custom when bishops still commanded respect. If, therefore, some families displayed my photo like a son who displays a photo of his parents in his room, it should be a sign that I fulfilled the role with which the Vatican charged me.

Even today, in my room and in my office, I have pictures of deceased Popes to whom I feel a filial attachment. Many ecclesiastics do the same. Are those Popes, too, guilty of the cult of personality? On the contrary, they were the very image of humility.

When one accepts a mission, one must do it thoroughly. Many, however, because of vanity, do not fulfill all their duties. Nevertheless, being recognized, respected and loved by the faithful are not the least among a bishop's duties, and such duty brings with it—whether one likes it or not—certain aspects of public renown.

Now, to recognize the usefulness of these aspects and to take on the duties which they bring really is a proof of humility. In Senegal, furthermore, the faithful would not have understood if anybody had reproached them for displaying the bishop's photo in a place of honor.

J.H.: So you think this is an aspect of humility when you insist on always wearing the pectoral cross and your bishop's ring, and expecting that the faithful kiss it on bended knees? Does it not rather show—as your opponents have it—the behavior of "a prewar bishop"?

M.L.: I think it part of my duties as a bishop not to camouflage myself in anonymity, which might make me forget my obligations, and to receive visible signs of respect. Those signs remind me of my mission to those whom the Church has entrusted to me. They should recognize me as children recognize their father.

The Island of Fadiouth

J.H.: But you were also the head of the Catholics in

Senegal as a demanding chieftain. Of this I convinced myself personally when I was at Fadiouth.

Fadiouth, as you well know, is a small island inhabited by river fishermen. In those times it was an extremely "picturesque" island; the huts were leaning one against the other, pigs trotted through the streets, and the half-naked fishermen were indescribably gentle. The Fathers of the Holy Spirit had set up a mission there which was really extraordinary: they had converted the entire population. Catholicism, in some way, had become a sort of state religion for those fishermen. The church of Fadiouth, a very nice church, given the poverty of these fishermen, was the only solid structure on the island. By habit, the fishermen, their wives and their children came to pray at all hours.

But on the day I landed in Fadiouth, the church was closed and the population behaved as if stricken by panic. They were talking about "a great misfortune." A few members of the population had committed grave sins and you punished the whole population by closing the church for one full week, forbidding the administration of the sacraments except for extreme unction (the rite of the dying).

Everyone's contrition and sadness affected me. Was it *necessary* for these Catholics to be pious and sensible, was it necessary for them to consider you their father, to experience such regret, to have incurred your reprimand and merited such punishment? I felt how uneasy they were. Did you not excessively punish these simple people?

M.L.: But no. They had committed acts of witchcraft, introduced by the Moslems.

To understand this, one has to know the framework in which the people of Fadiouth lived. Their whole island was Catholic. But the tributaries of the river were still peopled by Moslems who were outright proselytes and fetishists.

The only chance the people of Fadiouth had to retain their faith was to keep it strong and pure, so that they could be proud of it. And could they have been proud if that faith was constantly ridiculed without punishment? They would have been ashamed before the Moslems, who would have made fun of them.

On the contrary, when they found that the Catholics had a bishop capable of keeping them firmly on the path of religion, the Moslems experienced a surge of respect for them.

But explain this to a Frenchman who has never set foot into Senegal, in the fifties, in the bush! Where there is nothing but good common sense, people see an attack on the freedom to worship!

J.H.: Your explanation is certainly just, for I remember having been received by an iman and hearing him say: "The Catholics here have the chance of having a true head and of loving him. He really combines something that with us Moslems is very difficult to find: force and sweetness, severity and brotherliness."

This praise fits well with that of the African clergy who, at your departure, saluted you as a "great Senegalese." I have to add that the faithful of Fadiouth loved you, since they wrote you on your departure:

"We are so sorry to see you leave. We recognize how much your work in this village and all over Senegal was blessed by God. We promise, Excellency, to keep within our hearts the good example you gave us and all your teachings."

However, even though they comprehend your work in the Senegal in those days, the French Catholics incessantly repeat:

"Goodness! Archbishop Lefebvre still thinks he is living in the fifties in Africa! Therefore, when he cries out 'I don't want to become a Protestant,' he is still thinking of the wars of influence between the Catholic and the Protestant missions on African territory.

"And when he opposes religious freedom, he is still living in the times when he had to shield the faith of the people of Fadiouth against the Islamic temptations."

M.L.: That's true. My African experiences have left their mark on me. Providence has given me occasion to know the religious and political problems in Africa, especially on my visits as apostolic delegate, later as superior general of the Fathers of the Holy Spirit, functions which I always tried to carry out in the spirit of the Gospels. But these responsibilities did not permit me to make many observations and to draw from them important and useful conclusions. However, they showed me the danger of ecumenism for the faithful.

For example, you are talking about Protestantism, which seduced so many Catholics and toward which Vatican II—whether you like it or not—is oriented. Now, what was I able to observe about Protestantism? First of all, it is diffuse and vague. There are Lutherans, Calvinists, Episcopalians, Anglicans, etc. Protestants themselves complain about this division. But what is at the root of it, if not a badly understood spiritual liberty?

Unfortunately, this outburst menaces the conciliar Church, where so many priests on research, as it were, have come to "reunite" the faithful in functions, imparting to them not only their religious beliefs but also their political convictions, to form "little churches" which become more and more separated from each other.

In Africa, the dismembering of the Catholic Church and the "dialogue" with Moslems and Protestants have proved a disaster. Before the Council, the Church had made extraordinary progress in Africa. Her credit was high among all peoples, especially among Moslems. She had established a moral discipline which aroused respect because the Church dared proclaim that she was Truth. But starting from the moment when the impression was given that all faiths are of the same value and that the Catholic Church no longer possesses the only Truth, it brought the downfall of morals and the general dissolution of behavior.

The consequences are grave, especially where marriage is concerned. The return to polygamy makes it extremely difficult for priests to preserve the laws of the celibate. If things continue this way, one might come to a kind of voodoo religion, such as that among the blacks in Brazil. Or maybe to the triumph of Islam.

In the past, Islam lacked the power of expansion, especially in Africa. But lately it has advanced every day by conquering the fetishist populations. All the observers agree on this. How can such success be explained, unless Islam had been so confident in its principles at a time when Catholics, and priests too, do nothing but question their own faith?

This is the truth in 1977. If anyone wants to say that a Catholic bishop who regrets and condemns this situation is out of touch, then I am out of touch.

The Sermon of Lille

WHY NOT SIMPLY EXPLAIN THE GOSPEL?

J.H.: Now, Excellency, we have to take a jump over at least twenty years of your life, to talk about that sermon at Lille, a sermon which the press, radio and television have built up out of all proportion.

M.L.: I regret the enormous publicity about the Mass I celebrated at Lille and the sermon I preached during that Mass. For several months now I have asked myself if this was not the doing of Providence, who permitted it to happen to shake the faithful from their lethargy.

I was invited to Lille by the Group of the Association of Pius V, for a small circle. But then, a few weeks before the August 29 date, I received my "suspension *a divinis*" and another letter from the Pope. The telephone rang constantly: "Will Archbishop Lefebvre really go to Lille? Do you know what he will say? Will he be able to receive us?"

From Lille, they wrote me that they had to change the hall every few days to get a bigger one. Matters came to such a pass that I answered the journalists: "I won't go to Lille. It was you who made up this story, this pretended defiance of the Vatican. Well, this is quite simply resolved: I won't go." I had letters sent to all the organizers to have the Mass cancelled.

But finally, seeing that I could not prevent the people from coming, eight days before the date I began to think: "Since I cannot get out of this reunion which I have promised to attend, I may as well go. It is Providence who wants me to."

So it was the press—as always, in search of the sensational and the extraordinary—that entirely fabricated this "defiance."

In fact, if I had meant that Mass to be a publicity stunt, or planned to "maneuver my troops," as some said and wrote, I would have prepared that Mass long before and with extreme care. In Lille, I followed my custom and did not change a single word.

Without exception, I prepare my sermons according to a plan and I make notes, but I do not write them out sentence by sentence. This is the way I prepared my sermon at Lille. The ideas which I want to express are clear in my brain, but the expressions I find for them often are awkward. I don't pretend to be an orator. However, very rarely do I deviate from the framework which I have given myself. Besides, I count on the grace of the moment, which rarely fails when one only wants to proclaim the truth and encourage sanctity.

J.H.: But why, Excellency, did you not simply comment on the Gospel of the day?

M.L.: The faithful who came to Mass there expected me to shed some light on the present crisis in the Church and give them encouragement in their resolution to defend the faith at any cost. Should I have disappointed them?

J.H.: To get to the bottom of this, I have to tell you about a very curious experience, having just finished studying the complete text of your sermon. Even though the memory I had of it was that of a political speech, a reading seemed to clear up matters. You used a vocabulary which is difficult for modern ears, and this certainly because you were carried away by emotion, which had to be suppressed. Were you not, in the diocese where you had been ordained, the "rebel archbishop" maintained by 10,000 faithful?

M.L.: No, no—my emotions were not especially aroused. I was encouraged by the presence of such a mass of faithful and by their evident sympathy.

It is true, though, that today one cannot speak of the social reign of Our Lord Jesus Christ without immediately being accused of playing politics. But do we have to remain on the surface of the problem? I think it is necessary to go to the heart of the matter and dissect it with the help of the eternal verities, of which one of the first, and justly so, is the kingship of Our Lord Jesus Christ.

True, today the truth is not easily accepted. However, the applause from the faithful assembled in Lille proves that they expected me to proclaim the truth.

Did you think that the language Jesus Christ used was easily accepted by the Jews?

THE SOCIAL KINGDOM OF OUR LORD JESUS CHRIST

J.H.: Nevertheless, Excellency, if it is finally possible to understand the general sense of your homily, some people, we have to face it, are still doubtful about certain passages.

Speaking of the Council, you stated:

"What happened at the Council? By reading books, we learn about those who were instrumental in the changes in the Church, changes which happened before our eyes. Let us read, for instance, a word from *Le Catholicisme libéral* by Professor Prelot, the senator from Doubs. The author of this book writes:

" 'For a century and a half we have fought to make our opinions known within the Church but we never succeeded. Finally, Vatican II came and we triumphed. From now on, the theses and the principles of liberal Catholicism are officially accepted by the Church.'

"I am not saying this, the author does, and he does so gleefully. We, however, weep as we hear his words. For what have liberal Catholics wanted for a century and a half, but to marry the Church to the forces which destroy the family, forces which destroy religious and civic societies.

"This ill-starred marriage is, in effect, written into the Council. Take, for instance, the schema *Gaudium et Spes*. It advocates the marriage of principles of the Church with the principles of modern man. What else does it mean but uniting the Church, the Church of Our Lord Jesus Christ, with principles which are contrary to those of the Church and which undermine her!"

Furthermore, you have taken up the idea of dialogue, an idea which today—we can well say—has become the battle cry of Western society. And you exclaimed:

"Our Lord said: 'Go and teach all nations and convert them!' But he did not say: 'Start a dialogue with them and do not convert them!' He did not say so, because error and truth are not compatible; error and truth must not be placed on an equal footing. This would mean we put God and the devil on the same plane—the devil, who is father of every error; the devil, who is the father of lies!

"The charity the Gospel teaches us is the duty to proclaim this very truth to our brethren. Therefore, we must be missionaries, we must preach the Gospel to convert souls to God, and not start a dialogue with the weak, which would mean that we ourselves could be converted to error.

"Unfortunately, we know the result of the first dialogue of this kind: Eve's dialogue with the devil. Now Eve has put us all in the state of sin, because she held a dialogue with the devil. And now one wants to dialogue with the Freemasons: not only enter into a dialogue with them, but to permit Catholics to join Freemasonry. This is another abominable thing, for we know quite well that the practitioners of Freemasonry are strongly against Our Lord Jesus Christ.

"And the black masses that are going on, those horrible masses they celebrate, are a parody of the Mass of Our Lord. They seek to procure themselves consecrated Hosts, because they know that Our Lord Jesus Christ is in the Host, at least when our holy Mass is said according to the eternal rites. And we are supposed to start a dialogue with those people who are killing Our Lord Jesus Christ for the second time!"

Then you came to what one might term the "social" content of your homily:

"One no longer hears talk of a social reign of Our

Lord Jesus Christ, under the pretext that this is no longer possible. This I have heard from the mouth of the nuntio at Bern, from the mouth of the Vatican's messenger, Father Dhanis, former rector of the Gregorian University in Rome. When I told them that I was opposed to the Council, because ever since the Council the Vatican no longer upheld the idea of a Catholic state, they replied that actually there was no need any longer for a Catholic state, and that it was no longer possible.

"It is one thing to say that this is no longer possible, and another to establish this impossibility in principle. Now, then, what do we do with the 'Our Father,' which says 'Thy kingdom come, Thy will be done on earth as it is in heaven'? What lack of logic! Are we Christians or are we not? In truth, there will be no peace on earth, my dear brethren, except in the kingdom of Our Lord Jesus Christ.

"States are quarrelling, society is in crisis. And every day the newspapers, the radio and television urge us to make our industries more prosperous!

"Even from the standpoint of economics, it is necessary that Our Lord Jesus Christ should reign, because his kingdom follows from the principles of love and the Commandments, which bring balance to society and which establish justice and peace. Hence, my dear brethren, it is only under order, justice and peace that the economy can recover and flourish."

Finally, you spoke of Argentina in terms that first shocked me deeply.

All this was, of course, going to be interpreted as a revelation of antirepublican feelings and a resurgence of certain feelings of sympathy for the Action Française.

M.L.: This is absurd! You may as well say that Our Lord was of the Action Française. You must not fall into regrettable confusion. Well, let's get back to the points quoted. First, I want to take up again the schema of *Gaudium et Spes*, proposed by the Council, the spirit of which tended to merge the principles of the Church with the ideas of modern man. I have called this union adulterous. For a Catholic, this should be self-evident. To cite just one example: What are the ideas of modern man regarding marriage? That he can first try it, and then, after having entered into it, break it off. And the principles of the Church are that marriage is indissoluble. Where, I beg of you, do you see the Action Française in this? The weekly, *Le Sillon*, the worst enemy of Action Française, also defended the indissolubility of marriage in its pages.

Secondly, I said that error and truth are not compatible. This again seems self-evident, if not a truism.

Naturally, I stated that truth is on the side of Christ. Is that such an enormity for a Christian? Anyhow, if Catholics do not believe any longer that the truth is on the side of Jesus Christ, I ask myself how they dare call themselves Christians.

Maybe Charles Maurras, of Action Française fame, posed this question himself one day. I do not know, but if he did, I would say that Maurras had shown very good sense, at least in this matter.

Further, I castigated the spirit in which the conciliar

Church is now engaged in dialogue. To express myself better, I quoted Eve and the serpent, who, as you know, prepared a nice trap for Eve. Now, how many Catholics who are no longer taught the Bible are trapped every day in a great number of unwise dialogues, especially those steeped in atheistic Marxism? Is the Catholic who, after dialogue with a Communist, joins the party, the converted and conquered one?

I have spoken of Freemasonry in this connection. Whether you want to admit it or not, Freemasonry exists and, after a time of eclipse, it is developing its true spirit, and that, of course, is anti-Catholic. The danger here is great: on the one hand, the Freemasons present themselves more and more as "open"; on the other hand, the Catholics have less and less backbone and are less and less sure in their faith. They, too, risk being trapped by the Masonic spirit.

Once more: We are either Catholic or we are not. If we are, we think that the example and the teachings of Jesus Christ are divine, therefore unique. God did not become incarnate a second time. For me, this is sufficient proof: Every man who is imbued by the Gospel is at the same time a good son, a good husband, a good employee, a good artisan, a good mayor, a good deputy, a good minister, a good president of the republic. He loves his brethren and he is just, generous and courageous.

A nation composed of Christians could not be other than well-ordered, prosperous and compatible with its neighbors. It is in this sense that I am attached to the Catholic state. And why should the Catholic state be more utopian than the collective state? Should the

Catholic states that were born from Christian thought be considered inferior to the "democratic republics" born in the thought of Marx? Should the Vatican accept the representatives of the democratic states but reject the representatives of the Catholic state?

Finally, I also mentioned Argentina in the course of my homily. I had just been told that the situation there had improved and that the leaders were Catholic. I simply wanted to cite the example of a Catholic country which had again taken up Christian principles, the principles of the social kingdom of Our Lord Jesus Christ, and I tried to establish a cause and effect relation. I declare it with all my heart: I hope that this is exactly what it is all about.

I could—or should—have taken into account that, today, speaking of Argentina in particular and of South America in general, without disparaging them, means going against the grain of the most widely accepted ideas.

Does this mean that anarchy and disorder are normally accepted situations which our modern states should aim at? Besides, had I quoted Solzhenitsyn—that Christian who, after all, does not say anything I have not said already—would one not have immediately claimed that I am a bishop of the right?

5

Demythologizing Vatican II

The Pressure of the Mass Media

J.H.: Now, Excellency, we come to the time of Vatican II, that Council from which, as you say, all evil stems. It would have been different, in any case, if you had been listened to, even if only a little bit.

In the course of that Council, you made constant interventions. You did this with force and, for the most part, also in the name of a group of bishops who showed a great deal of wisdom and great spirituality.

Those bishops shared your opinion that the Council, to their great sadness and concern, had been diverted from its aim by a "brain trust" of modernistic Council Fathers, advised by very "involved" theologians and, to no small degree, supported by the press. The Council met from 1962 to 1965, a time when journalists of the written and spoken media specialized in religious questions and pushed with all their might for a change. In any case, they applauded the avant-garde theologians.

One was free to assume that all Catholics shared their beliefs, because the majority of them, dazzled by their demonstrations, did not dare refute them, even if they seemed to go against their religious feelings or, simply, against good sense.

It seems, therefore, that the Council Fathers, who had called upon the Holy Spirit to enlighten them, but who were only men and, like everybody else, susceptible to rumors, were conditioned by the information media. It was consequently easy for the group of whom I am speaking, and who are extremely intelligent, to occupy the "strategic" points, to infiltrate and lead the Council where they wanted.

I myself can pass no judgment on the underlying purpose of this undertaking. I would like to believe that the prelates who were to guide the Church thought in good faith that the Church would be rejected by the world, if it would not slowly adapt itself.

But in view of the facts, I think I should note here that your three-year-long battle, inch by inch, against the reforms of the Vatican was a battle lost before it started, since the bishops who shared your opinions were in the minority.

In addition, in the "conditioning process" which developed, you were certainly painted in the most unfavorable colors. One tried—with all the oratorical amenities intact—to throw doubt on your capabilities. One even insinuated that you were a theologian of only modest range and little qualified. Then, the last strokes were added to the picture by stating that your stay in Africa, where you spent so many years, would not have made it possible for you to know of the progress in the modern world and to adapt yourself. This was pure slander, because it was this very apostolate in Africa, and especially the episcopal conferences which you had to establish, which put you well in touch with the questions posed by the Church.

You see, this is really all of one piece: Since they could not attack you otherwise, your enemies shed doubt upon your qualifications. As far as your knowledge of theology is concerned, your doctorate from the Gregorian University should have assured them, for if the faculty of that university does not consist of the best theologians, who forms them? The opinion of a remarkable specialist, Abbot Berto, is likewise convincing. He wrote about you in the middle of the Council: "A theologian? Please God that all the Fathers would be to the degree that he is."

M.L.: I want to inject a remark.

The importance of the group of Council Fathers to which I belonged was, contrary to what you just said, at least equal to the active group of liberals. But the latter had the overwhelming advantage of being backed by authority which permitted them to have all their new theses endorsed. Anyhow, I personally counted little in that battle. You made a mistake in putting me in the center of things.

A Great Hope Disappointed

J.H.: One thing is sure: The dawning of the Council was the object of great hopes for you. Many Fathers have testified that you arrived in Rome with great expectations and joy in your heart.

M.L.: Yes, of course! It was certainly not with a closed mind or a mind "crystallized in the past" that I approached what I considered a great event in the life of the Church. And I expected that there were to be changes and adaptations to be carried out. I was so convinced of this that, on March 25, 1965, I addressed a long letter to the Fathers of the Holy Spirit, whose superior general I was. In regard to the expected evolution, I wrote them, for example: "Let me say unhesitatingly that certain liturgical reforms are necessary and that it is to be wished that the Council continue in this manner."

I added: "But later on we have to pause, because it is inconceivable that we should change missals, breviaries and rituals every ten years. It is inconceivable, likewise, that one constantly changes the texts and the official translations."

Was this not reasonable? And does not the galloping evolution of the liturgy today show *a posteriori* that I was right? This is what the Conference of Bishops of France came to recognize in their meeting at Lourdes—but ten years too late! The wrong was already done.

Yes, I repeat it, I approached Vatican II with high hopes and a very open mind. I had no doubt that our prayers, together with those of the faithful all over the world, would make of this Council an occasion of great progress for the Church.

But the Central Preparatory Commission roused serious doubts in me. The clash between Cardinal Ottaviani and Cardinal Bea at their last commission meeting augured nothing good. My anxieties were borne out by the experience of the first few sessions of the Council. By and by, my fears took shape and increased.

My enemies are right when they say that I signed certain documents which I am now repudiating.

I should have battled more vigorously, perhaps, for an improvement of the texts, or refused to sign them, as I subsequently did with others.

In reality, I was hoping against hope that the Holy Spirit would prevent certain projects from coming to pass or that the Pope would intervene at the last moment. This, at any rate, was the opinion of the Fathers who held on to tradition. But session after session it became clear that the Council was not going to be what one had wished and that it would constitute an immense danger to the Church.

J.H.: Excellency, we are not going to retrace the history of Vatican II; countless books have done so. But I would like to enumerate here the points on which you refused to cede and to examine the working conditions of the Council Fathers.

M.L.: These working conditions were very difficult. In fact, they would have liked us to give our agreement, from start to finish, to the proposed texts without any debate. Thus, right from the start of the Council on October 20, 1963, we had a quarter of an hour—yes, I said a quarter of an hour!—to give our opinion on the first message, a message of great importance because the Fathers would address themselves to the entire world!

This message, undoubtedly edited by French experts of the avant-garde, Father Congar among them, already harbored ideas which were to corrupt the Council. It appealed to a "spiritual renewal from which would come a happy momentum for the benefit of all human values: scientific discovery, technical progress, the spread of culture, etc."

The demagogic directions of that text were clear. The confusion which resulted between spiritual and human values was full of danger. It provoked my first intervention. I stated especially:

"In my humble opinion, this message considers, above all, human and temporal goods and very little of spiritual and eternal ones. It addresses itself mostly to the good of the earthly city, and too little to the heavenly city toward which we strive and for which we are on earth. It is true, people expect from us, because of our exercise of the Christian virtues, the improvement of their own temporal condition; but much more they desire, even on this earth, spiritual and supernatural values. It is in these values that we find peace and beatitude."

But nobody paid attention to this intervention, one of the rare ones concerned with this subject. Its consequence, however, became evident: from that day on the liberals distrusted me and the leaders of the French episcopate tried to isolate me even more as that "traditionalist" who was trying to upset the applecart.

A Dogmatic or a Pastoral Council?

A month later, I had the impression that everything was kept cryptic on purpose—and this undoubtedly for the purpose of having the texts accepted first which were apparently harmless, but whose direction was destined to lead the Council Fathers later on to vote in favor of the most harmful documents.

I was afraid that I knew what this meant: to have questionable documents accepted under the pretext that they were only "pastoral" and to appeal later, at the end of the Council, to the ego of the Fathers, that Vatican II, just as the Council of Trent, must be dogmatic, which would give the force of law to the questionable texts. On November 27, 1962, I made my second intervention, a perfectly clear proposal which every logical mind would have to agree to.

Why did we come together? What was this meeting all about? On the one hand, to reply to the hopes of His Holiness Pope John XXIII, who had just told us: "It is of the utmost importance for an ecumenical council to preserve and to form in the most effective manner the sacred deposit of Christian doctrine." On the other hand, to reply to another call of the Pope: Had he not reminded us of the necessity to spread the Gospel through the world and to all human beings, regardless of their intelligence or their knowledge?

I therefore remarked that we have to follow these two aims: On the one hand, to "express the doctrine in a dogmatic and scholarly way for theologians and above all for the professors in the seminaries" and on the other hand, "to represent the truth in a most pastoral manner for the formation of all the faithful."

I declared:

"Each Council commission should prepare two documents: one, more dogmatic, for the use of theologians, the other, pastoral, for the use of the faithful Catholics, or even non-Catholics, and, even more, the unbelievers.

"In doing so, the dogmatic documents, worked out with so much care and useful in presenting the truth to our dear priests and especially to professors and theologians, will always remain the golden rule of faith.

"Thus the pastoral documents which could be translated much more easily into the different national languages could, in a way more understandable to them, represent truth to all men at home with the profane sciences but not with theology.

"With what gratitude would all men receive the light of the truth from the Council!"

As you see, I said that the pastoral documents would be prepared so that they could easily be translated into the different national languages, which nullifies the charge, often levelled at me, that I want to "imprison and petrify the faith in Latin."

Nevertheless, I believe sincerely that the Council could have been quite different. It would have really been essentially "dogmatic."

But the progressives and the liberals like to live in a climate of ambiguity. It would have annoyed them extremely to clarify the aims of the Council. They had my proposal rejected after declaring: "The Council is not a dogmatic Council, but a pastoral one. We do not want to redefine dogma but to expose truth pastorally!"

This is what they said at the beginning of the Council. And thus the Council was in effect a uniquely pastoral one. But look how, ten years later, the maneuver which I foresaw is unfolding. The Council has become "dogmatic," and whoever considers it "pastoral" is a heretic or schismatic!

J.H.: This seems to me a sleight of hand!

The Primacy of the Pope

One of the most striking reproaches made of you concerns your flagrant disobedience of the Pope. Is this disobedience in direct contrast to your stand? At the Council you yourself fought for maintaining the supremacy of the Vicar of St. Peter.

M.L.: Yes, I fought against the "collegiality" which the liberals and the progressives, in their horror of what they call "personal power," wanted to establish in order to undermine the authority which always belonged to the Pope and which St. Thomas Aquinas defined by declaring "the best government is that of one head." But the progressives and the liberals scoff about St. Thomas Aquinas. In any case, their "collegiality" was fraught with menace for the Church. That's what I said in the name of several Council Fathers during my third intervention in October of 1963. I do not, to this day, regret one word of that intervention:

"Several Fathers have spoken about the menace of diminishing the power of the papacy, and we are completely in agreement with them. But we perceive another danger, possibly even worse: the progressive and menacing disappearance of the essential power of the bishops, namely that they are 'true pastors who, each of them, care for and govern properly, effectively and in keeping with their office their own flock entrusted to them.'

"Soon, and imperceptibly, the national assemblies of bishops, with their commissions, will tend and govern all the flocks, in such a manner that the priests and the faithful will find themselves placed between these two pastors: the bishop, whose authority is theoretical, and the assembly of bishops, which will actually exercise all power."

This intervention was very badly received by the liberals. But since several Fathers had intervened in the same sense, the Holy Father appended to the conciliary text an explanatory note which on a separate line showed the traditional doctrine. But unfortunately, with the spirit of Vatican II, what happened was that the liberals and the progressives returned to the charge and slyly slipped in *de facto* what they had not been able to obtain *de jure*.

Thus, there is no contradiction between my position at the Council and my present one. On the contrary! Besides, I am convinced that the censure of Econe is a consequence of what I denounced that time in my intervention. The council of bishops in some country, with a small majority, could actually checkmate the will of the Holy Father or force him to take up sanctions which he himself deems unjust.

And what is worse in this matter—those who most strongly fought the supremacy of the Pope are now placing it above all others in order to condemn me even more surely.

The bishops who are today so often contradicted by the younger members of their clergy may find out how much the liberals and the progressives have harmed the Church by sapping their authority, as they did that of the Pope.

ABOUT RELIGIOUS LIBERTY

J.H.: One of your fiercest battles, Excellency, took place about ecumenism and religious liberty. In this, as your enemies say, you showed yourself "particularly conservative, even reactionary."

M.L.: We could discuss this for hours, as it was done at the Council, but the die was already cast, if I may say so.

In brief, two schemas had been worked out by the Preparatory Commission even before the Council started. One, titled *On Religious Tolerance*, was prepared by Cardinal Ottaviani. This was a beautiful document, very close to the traditional doctrine.

The other was presented by Cardinal Bea. It bore the title *On Religious Liberty*, and, to my mind as well as to those of a number of other Fathers, it contained untenable statements and even gross errors with regard to the truth of the eternal Church.

For example: Whereas the Church, as always, proclaims that there is no salvation except in Jesus Christ, Cardinal Bea stated that every man, simply following his conscience, could find eternal salvation.

There were many remarks and observations to be made. The following come to my mind:

"It is one thing to state the need for greater liberty from authority; it is another to pretend that this sort of thing conforms better to human dignity. Such pretension would imply admitting the right to scandal, either by error or by vice. God save us from this."

And another: "A mistaken internal religion often leads to external acts of superstition, contrary to human dignity and divine dignity. A misinterpreted religion inevitably brings with it principles which are contrary to the natural law."

Don't you think that these observations are correct?

Unfortunately, His Holiness John XXIII, who had opened the Council and of whose declining powers the liberals and progressives had taken advantage, was soon to be called before God. Paul VI was chosen by the Conclave and we hoped that he would soon take things in hand. Thus, in June of 1964, four other Fathers and I sent a letter demanding the opportunity to scrutinize the proposed schemas. We wrote:

"In the wording of these schemas, we do not find at all what His Holiness John XXIII had asked us, that is, exactness of terms and concepts which made for the particular glory of the Council of Trent and of the First Vatican Council. Confusion in style and ideas produces a constant impression of ambiguity."

And we added: "We do not want to be officious, but we sincerely want to work for the salvation of souls. And we want to add that a great many faithful and priests are sincerely troubled."

This letter was followed by a detailed note, prepared by Cardinal Larraona and signed by many Fathers. It contained most of our observations. Unfortunately, Paul VI replied to the cardinal by a demurrer, and in terms which filled us with fear for the future. For him, the important points of the note were "assertions . . . supported by questionable arguments." Above all, he questioned, in a manner which must be called offensive, the intellectual honesty of Cardinal Larraona and the cosigners of the note. He wrote:

"We have reasons to believe, after what we have been told, that the sending of the document is due principally to your initiative, Cardinal Larraona, and that even those who signed it did not have a complete and well-considered knowledge of it."

It is this "after what we have been told," to support a false accusation, which showed that the new Pope did not rely completely on his conscience, and that the progressives and the liberals were already weighing heavily in his thinking. They were already exercising great influence over him. And that is the reason why we continued the fight to the last day of the Council: for the honor of the Church of Our Lord Jesus Christ, and that it should not be said by future generations that there were not at least some voices raised at Vatican II to refute the pernicious ideas.

THE CHURCH AND THE MODERN WORLD

Among the many other interventions which I made, I want to mention the one which had as its aim the "Pastoral Constitution on the Church in the Modern World."

According to this schema, many of the questions of our times have gone unanswered by the Church. It was therefore necessary to work out answers adequate for our times.

This was absolutely wrong, however. The Church has always responded to all the questions. This was the manner in which the Council was conducted: to barter the replies of the eternal Church against the agreeable answers of the progressives and the liberals. That is, for the perversions of the modern world.

This I made clear in the most explicit manner. "Those who demand from the Church replies to the questions of our modern times are looking precisely for answers already given by the Church but they refuse to admit it, I am afraid. Like some Catholic—and non-Catholic—writers, they raise their voices in order to speak. Those famous people of 'today's world' find and invent a mass of questions, so that the Church might contradict its traditional doctrine!

"The vocation of the human person, the family, marriage, social and economic relations among men, civil societies, peace, militant atheism—are these really new questions for the Church? Who dares to say so?

"Would it not scandalize all priests if we shrug off all the brilliant teachings of so many Sovereign Pontiffs, published for centuries, now that we come to grips with the same reality, the same subject matter? Let us never forget that the Roman Church is our Mother and our Mistress, according to the saying: 'Rome has spoken; the case rests.'

"Let us be careful: If we keep silent about the teachings of the Church, this silence will go down in the eyes of the entire world as a lapse in devotion and piety toward our Mother and Mistress, and not without grave damage to the universal Church.

" 'Honor thy father and thy mother, and you will be blessed.' I have spoken."

But the progressives and the liberals who dominated the Council did not take any notice of my statements and during the fourth session of the Council in September, 1965, I had to come back to the question of the Church and the modern world. I did this in a precise and complete way, showing that, in a great many passages of the proposed document, principles were backed which are in flagrant contradiction to the traditional doctrine of the Church—not to mention the ambiguous and dangerous ones and the omissions.

A simple example will show you that this document, which seemed composed in order to ruin the Church forever, revealed such grievous imperfections that it should have been rejected in its entirety.

Page five and passim read:

"Today, more than before, all the inhabitants of the earth, regardless of race, color, social origin or religion, must recognize that all men have a common destiny, in adversity as in good times, that all must take the same path toward a goal until now only glimpsed through shadows."

What goal? Had *anyone* ever seen a Council, or Fathers of the Church, or bishops with a mandate to show the path Jesus Christ wants men to follow defined in this way—toward a goal "only glimpsed through shadows"?

This was the reason why I declared with the utmost force:

"This pastoral constitution is neither pastoral nor does it come from the Catholic Church. It does not nourish men and Christians with evangelical and apostolic truth. Nor has the Church ever spoken like this.

"We cannot listen to this voice, for it is not the voice of the Bride of Christ. This voice is not the voice of the spirit of Jesus Christ, for we know the voice of our Shepherd; we recognize it. That voice we do not. The clothes are those of the sheep but the voice is not that of the Shepherd, but maybe of the wolf. I have spoken."

As you can see, my judgment about the Council was not formed yesterday. Even before the closing of the Council, I proclaimed to all the Fathers assembled there that, according to my view, it was not the Holy Spirit who inspired the Council but possibly Satan.

In any case, against our implacable opposition, the Pope had two statements affixed to the documents concerning truth in the Church and conformity to traditional doctrine. But the spirit of what was to become the declaration "On Religious Liberty" was not changed in the least by it.

A Year Later

I made two more interventions, but the Council was winding down. One would soon be able to measure the effects of the evil done by the progressives and the liberals. Hardly a year after Vatican II, the faith of so many Catholics was shaken to such an extent that Cardinal Ottaviani asked all the bishops in the world and all the superior generals of orders and congregations to reply to an inquiry on the dangers that certain fundamental truths were encountering at the moment.

I answered with a long letter on December 20, 1966, enumerating the ravages the Council had already wrought, especially pertaining to relaxed morals. I wrote:

"Driven to the wall by these facts, one has to conclude that the Council has favored the spread of liberal errors to an incredible extent. Faith, morals, ecclesiastical discipline are shaken to their roots, as predicted by all the Popes.

"The destruction of the Church advances with giant strides, because of the exaggerated authority given to the Conference of Bishops; the Pope has rendered himself powerless. In one year, what painful examples! But in the meantime, the successor of Peter, and he alone, can save the Church.

"I hope that the Holy Father will surround himself with vigorous defenders of the faith, that he will assign them to the important dioceses, that he may consider publishing important documents, proclaiming the truth, persecuting and correcting error, without fear of contradictions, without fear of schism, without fear of derailing pastoral purposes of the Council.

"The Holy Father might consider:

"Encouraging the bishops to reestablish faith and individual morals in their respective dioceses, as it behooves a good shepherd;

"Backing up the courageous bishops and urging them to reform their seminaries and restore the study of St. Thomas Aquinas;

"Encouraging the superior generals to maintain in

the novitiates of their communities the fundamental principles of all Christian ascesis, above all, obedience;

"Encouraging the establishment of Catholic schools, the insistence on sound doctrine, and Christian family associations;

"Finally, reprimanding the architects of errors and reducing them to silence."

This is what I wrote ten years ago to Cardinal Ottaviani, which the Vatican never acknowledged. Here is what all the bishops of France should have done in the course of ten years which have passed since Vatican II. But they have been silent. They permitted errors to develop, permitted the progressives and liberals to undermine the Church, even if they themselves did not lend a hand to the destruction.

And here, after having condemned me, they assemble at Lourdes and finally state the damages—and they condemn me, at least implicitly, in the name of Vatican II, which has done so much evil.

THE CASE OF CARDINAL LIENART

J.H.: Before I have to conclude the conversation about the Council, I want to make a remark and subsequently ask a few more questions.

It is clear that your attachment to the Church eternal, your irremovable faith, your certitudes and, if I may dare say so, your mysticism have led you—as they will always lead you—to express your convictions in a direct manner to which it is sometimes difficult to adhere.

Thus, on Pentecost 1965, in the middle of the Council, you wrote, concerning the schema on religious liberty:

"Truth, faced with error, is itself intolerant, just as health is opposed to malady. The magisterium cannot permit the right to religious liberty, even if it tolerates it. God has actually not given to man the right to choose his religion, but only the unhappy possibility, which is a weakness of humanity."

We understand that this language was dealt a rebuttal!

You have expressed yourself in a unique manner on the level of spirit and soul, and those who know you also know you will never, in any way, confuse the requirements of your faith and the demands of charity which make you so friendly toward all men, whoever they may be. That notwithstanding, that writing was grist to the mills of your opponents. It was only too easy for them to say that you were "a dangerous heir of the Inquisition."

As to questions: the main one has to do with the manner in which you think the Council was maneuvered by those whom certain people call a "lobby" of liberal and progressive bishops.

It has been said and repeated, and you yourself have let it be understood, that those bishops, mostly from France, Germany, Switzerland and the Benelux countries, banded together to put a veritable stranglehold on the Council. It is insinuated (when it is not said so categorically) that some of them were allied to

Freemasonry and that, of course, for one aim only: to destroy the Church. The same rumors say that Cardinal Lienart himself was a Freemason. And here is a book, just published, favorable to you, which tells us that Paul VI—as if this were possible—was tied or is tied to Freemasonry, and that his origins make him a "double" agent.

I say it as it is: even if it should have happened that a cardinal, who is wielding great influence, is, or was, connected with Freemasonry, all these attacks and insinuations to me seem defamatory and extremely unpleasant. Besides, as far as I know, Freemasonry has its own goals, which do not seem to have anything to do with the destruction of the Church.

M.L.: I have asked myself over and over again: Why were these bishops and His Holiness Paul VI able to give their own directions to the Council or accept those orientations? I am not the only one to ask these questions, and some of them, I think, were able to supply the answer which you have just expressed.

But, even if I happened to hit on this answer, I refuse to be drawn into this territory, because I do not think I am sufficiently informed.

But what is really serious about the pre-Council, the Council and the post-Council period is that all those people worked as if their aims would be identical with those of Freemasonry. The fact is that all this was accomplished by a group of bishops, able to impose on others what they had decided upon.

Cardinal Lienart, for his part, played an important role at the beginning of the Council by acting so that the preparatory documents should not form the basis of our work. Yet these documents, whose preparation had taken two years, had been prepared with utmost care and a great respect for tradition.

However, Cardinal Lienart had favored the appointment of liberal prelates to key positions on the Council, especially in the commissions.

This attitude of the cardinal, who ordained me and consecrated me a bishop and whom, as I told you, I regarded as my spiritual father, has given me much pain.

J.H.: It seems to me, Excellency, that the enemies of the cardinal wanted to be oversubtle. We have to believe, I think, that Cardinal Lienart was a man of a certain age, who, at the start of his episcopate, when he was still a young man, was considered "a red bishop."

I imagine that he wanted to show that old age has not changed his avant-garde spirit. It was a kind of ostentation which made him put this tendency at the service of some of his most progressive colleagues.

As to these colleagues: for an explanation of their attitudes, you have to take into account the conscious or even unconscious but overriding sentiments apparent in the Catholic faithful of the West, who are more or less jealous of Rome's prerogatives and are often prompted to call the Vatican retrogressive. It was the case of now or never. Especially since the new ideas rampant in Germany, the Benelux countries and elsewhere, much more active than in France, had greatly impressed him. This is for me, quite simply, the explanation for Vatican II.

Now that the Demon had one or the other supports

right there, it was another story: evil as he is, he could have found himself, on one or the other occasion, right in the middle of preceding councils.

M.L.: Only God knows what really went on during Vatican II, and what were the true motivations of those who brought their weight to bear on the Council. Without having to say so, I wish your explanation were the right one. This explanation, at any rate, recognizes that the Holy Spirit, finally, was absent from a Council where every day one saw its damaging effects.

TROUBLING FACTS

J.H.: Many troubling facts have been reported. It is, for instance, said that Pope VI took off his tiara as he entered the Council, probably to demonstrate that he accepted collegiality. Besides, it is said that he never wears his tiara.

M.L.: It is true that the action of the Pope, taking off his tiara and putting it up for sale for the poor, left us all flabbergasted. Did he give up that particular tiara, or did he give up for good wearing the tiara? The second alternative, the true one, is really very serious.

J.H.: People also talk about the very uncharitable, the awful incident on October 30, 1962, involving Cardinal Ottaviani.

The cardinal, at seventy-two and half blind, fought on that day for tradition, and especially to save the

Mass of Pius V which the progressives wanted to dismantle. He said:

"You cannot treat the rites of the Holy Mass like a piece of cloth which one can wear differently according to the fashion of the times, according to the fancy of each generation."

He was intent on providing a lengthy explanation, but it had been decided that no intervention could last longer than ten minutes. Those were quickly over. The subject was the Mass and it was Ottaviani who was speaking, one of the most illustrious servants of the Church and one of the oldest. But this did not keep Cardinal Alfrink, a member of the liberal group, who presided over the session, from tinkling his bell.

The orator, who was a bit hard of hearing, did not hear the bell and continued with his explanation. Then Cardinal Alfrink had the microphone cut off. Cardinal Ottaviani continued to speak, accompanying his words with eloquent gestures. But nobody heard anything; it looked like a silent film. A tremendous fit of laughter shook the Council Fathers, so loud that the cardinal could not help but understand, and he sat down.

M.L.: Yes, this happened exactly as you told it. I was ashamed for the bishops who behaved in such a deplorable manner toward one of the best among them.

Such things are like a curse. They are certainly causing the blindness which has struck the bishops today.

How could one believe in the presence of the Holy Spirit under such conditions?

6

The Fruits of the Council

THE BEGINNING

J.H.: You have spoken out vigorously, Excellency, against the liberal ideas of a group of bishops, who came for Vatican II. But did you already foresee that the faithful and the ecclesiastics would interpret the new texts so badly as to adopt attitudes and profess beliefs which were outright dangerous to the Church, even to faith and morals? Did you already imagine that thousands of priests would abandon their flocks? That others would approve of trial marriage?

Or, what is worse, that a Catholic faculty, like the one at the Flemish University of Louvain in Belgium, would experiment with the temporary sterilization of women, not only a scandalous religious aberration but also, very likely, a scandalous defiance of medical ethics?

M.L.: Well, surely at the moment when I rose against certain directions the Council was taking, I did not foresee the consequences very clearly. But history teaches us that the moment we acknowledge false principles, we are opening Pandora's box of unforeseen consequences. Nevertheless, one does not trifle with the objectives of marriage, as the declaration of "The Church and the Modern World" leads us to assume.

The most modest of jurists know this: if the laws are not clear there always is one, then ten, then 10,000 citizens to make them say what they did not say, and finally to make fun of them.

The example of the medical faculty of the University of Louvain is a case in point. There are Christian physicians who behave like most of their atheistic colleagues would not even dare to. Had there not been a Vatican II, would they have behaved in that manner?

Actually, as the new religious ideas of Vatican II began to play a greater role in mundane affairs, these Catholic doctors were quite naturally searching for means to adjust carnal desires to the laws of the Church in what concerns the transmission of life.

The conscious and premeditated misinterpretation is diabolic, but who has opened the door to Satan?

Fortunately, the majority of physicians worthy of their name refuse to change anything in the Oath of Hippocrates, which obliges them to respect and defend life everywhere. Since their position sheds light on mine, I want to add a few words.

One wonders often why the practitioners utilize all their scientific skill and techniques to prolong life in those who are already fatally ill. Why do they do it?

First, they do not want to stand in the way of a "miracle," even if the chances to see complete improvement are nil. But mostly because on the day that they agree to ease the death of a patient whose brain is gone, they would risk acting the same way toward the patient whose suffering is excruciating, then toward the one whose moans annoy the family. By and by, they might come to exterminate the handicapped, the feeble, and finally to practice euthanasia, already close to legalization in certain states of North America.

The same conditions apply to the religious sector, where every attack on the sacred risks the desacralization of the entire world of religion. I am therefore certain that some of the effects of the Council are deplorable.

I say "some of the effects" because not everything in the Council was bad. But my anxiety is mounting, because all the documents carry the mark of a new spirit which is far removed from the true spirit of the Church.

Unfortunately, that fear was well grounded. Those bishops who are the most hostile to traditionalism recognize it implicitly, even if they talk otherwise; we are witnessing a general spiritual upheaval.

Cardinal Marty has recently published some significant views in *Vie Catholique*. The cardinal tells the faithful that we must not exaggerate, but, nevertheless, he writes:

"It is true that there is a general uneasiness that a great number of Catholics experience. . . . There are excesses; we have made mistakes. . . . I know that some priests just improvise certain eucharistic prayers. The mystery of the Eucharist, which is nobody's property, is reduced to the dimensions of the celebrant's inspiration.

"I deplore a certain sectarianism. We sometimes meet people with an arsenal of preconceived ideas. We get caught up in ideologies. The danger of a certain neo-clericalism exists. Some have taken the liberty, under the aegis of Vatican II, to say or to do whatever they wish or to act on their personal opinions."

Unfortunately, the cardinal does not ask: Whose fault is it? Such a question, undoubtedly, would be a departure from the spirit of defending the Council—a lax spirit which is responsible for the fact that, as time goes on, the label "Catholic" may embody perversions which can only be the works of Satan.

Cardinal Marty recognizes, though always implicitly, that many disheartened Catholics have left the Church, saying: "The Church is in the winter of its life." He adds:

"We must not lose heart before this apparent death of nature: Winter is also the season for germination, for expectation and hope, for apostolic work."

I think that this winter we are talking about is very severe, responsible for death, not life. Why not be more watchful of the planting and the growth? Why not recognize that life flourishes in such seminaries as Econe, where we are trying precisely to produce life-giving fruits—the true sacrifice of the Mass, prayer, penitence and the true teachings of the Church?

Cardinal Marty and the French bishops who recognize today that they have failed could have opened their eyes much sooner. If they had done so, they might have prevented many faithful from leaving the Church.

J.H.: Certainly, Excellency! But it is always pleasant for a man, especially a bishop, to see that events have proved him right, even if the events are deplorable. People are consequently asking themselves, when you fulminate so vehemently against post-conciliar errors, if you are not animated by this "I told you so" satisfaction, which, as your enemies see it, is a sign of old age.

M.L.: Old age or not, the facts are here for everybody to see. I will quote here only a statement by

Father Garrigou-Lagrange. One could dedicate it to all the progressives whose ignorance equates traditionalism with pessimism. Here is what he says:

"The young professors often teach more than they know. The middle-age professors teach everything they know and the old professors teach what is useful for the formation of the spirit: the principles and their most important consequences."

The evidence is in. Vatican II, in its desire to be young and modern, to meet the world, has applied false principles. We can see the results every day. We must therefore fight everywhere for the faith, that is, denounce the consequences, recall the true principles, principles which hold for all times and under all conditions.

A TIME OF WAR

The fight for the faith is unrelenting and it is for this that the Church here on earth is called the "Militant Church." But the enemy is not always active; there are also calm periods. That is not the case today; the Church is torn apart. While there are times when all we have to do is to be watchful, there are also times when we must fight, because to fight is indispensable for survival. As it says in Ecclesiastes:

All things have their season . . .
A time to be born and a time to die,
A time to weep and a time to laugh.

This goes on, but my favorite verses, to which I want to draw special attention, are:

A time to keep silent and a time to speak.
A time to embrace and a time to shun embraces.
A time to rend and a time to sew.
A time of love and a time of hatred.
A time of war and a time of peace.

It has been repeatedly said of me that I do not want to understand anything, that I am hardheaded, that my language is too strong, that I lack charity toward my brethren and humility toward the Vatican.

God will judge, if errors were committed in the defense of the faith. But when those who remain faithful to the Holy Mass are sanctioned severely, and we have to close our eyes to the many "eucharistic celebrations," which sometimes are nothing but a communal meal of politicized groups, is this a time for embraces?

When Bishop Puech, bishop of Carcassonne, refused to conduct the funeral of a priest, a refugee in his diocese from the East, who had become the chaplain in a religious school and a friend of the whole population, according to the formal vow of that priest, that is, according to the rite of St. Pius V, is that peace?

When the Vatican makes Pope Paul VI sign a seventeen-page-long typewritten report, in which I am ordered to return to St. Siège and to their respective dioceses the seminarians and the priories of the Priestly Fraternity of St. Pius X, is this a time to mend?

Besides, what would the dioceses in question do with our seminarians and our priories, except to sell them, as they had sold the majority of the buildings which they owned before, because of lack of faithful, lack of priests, lack of contributions which even the poorest made to the clergy, when they deserved their trust? What would the thousands upon thousands of Catholics, who help us, say if their sacrifice, taken penny by penny out of their income, would be detoured from its goal?

We should remember Pascal's commentary regarding the passage in Ecclesiastes which we just mentioned. Pascal says first: "It would go against the aims of peace, if the state permitted foreigners to enter in order to pilfer it, without resisting them for fear of disturbing the peace," and further: "Thus, in the Church, when the truth is offended by enemies of the faith, when one sees it torn from the hearts of the faithful so that error can reign in them, to remain at peace, does that mean serving the Church or betraying her? Does it mean to defend her or to undermine her?"

There is thus a time when peace is just and another when it is unjust. It is written that there are times of war and times of peace, but it says nothing of times of peace and times of error. On the contrary, it is written that God's truth is eternal.

I pray every day from the depth of my heart that the time may come to mend and to embrace, the time of peace. But in the meantime, what else can the true Catholics do but defend their faith in eternal truth?

Do We Have the Right?

J.H.: I don't have to tell you, Excellency, that the best defense still is attack. But here the Christian runs the risk of a lack of charity. In this regard, the latest book by Michel de St. Pierre, which is full of gossip, is a poor example. Even if the facts are deplorable, it is possible that the author or authors mean well. When one picks out an isolated fact, it often means to elicit one of the bad sides of the human spirit, that which never ceases to generalize. Personally, I am quite sure that the majority of the clergy does not follow the aberrations of a few. A great many priests lead a difficult but pure life in the light of the Gospel. Does one have the right to include them, without distinction, in the act of accusation?

M.L.: Apparently not. But, if there were no courageous Christians to point out the error and to proclaim the truth, might the good priests not be contaminated in turn?

It was you, I think, who told me of the meeting which took place after the First Communion of one of your sons. The preparation for this First Communion consisted mostly in making winged deer, which symbolized the ascent toward Christ. Unfortunately, it rained on the day they should have been released and the flying deer did not come off successfully.

During a meeting between the parents and the pastor of that parish, you said, you had spoken your mind. You had given him a piece of your mind on that. The astonished pastor appealed to the other parents, hoping that they would hear him out. But they replied:

"We kept silent, so we would not be regarded backward. But since one among us has found the courage of his conviction, we too want to say with him: Yes; we share his views."

Finally, the pastor admitted: "Actually, I am really on your side. But whenever I am at clergy meetings I observe that they are all in favor of the new methods. Finally, I have to tell myself that the Holy Spirit is with them and I follow."

This anecdote proves that Catholics, with due respect to those who mostly are of good faith, have the duty to denounce, loudly and clearly, the mistakes of the conciliar Church.

If more than one hundred young people in the seminary of Econe had not had the courage to testify to their faith in the eternal Church, and to stand up under the fulminations of the Vatican, the unrest of a great many Catholics would never have surfaced. The bishops continue to deny that there is uneasiness.

CATECHESIS

J.H.: Let us now review some of the fruits of the Council. We may start with catechesis. Better than anything, it shows the truth of the old proverb that one bad apple spoils the barrel. The future of countless boys and girls often depends on one single individual—don't you think so? Abusive generalizations aside, don't we have to admit that good Catholic parents often complain bitterly about religious teaching in our schools today?

M.L.: To be sure! And you will immediately see the misleading spirit of our times, which releases torrents of words in order to appear superior to the spirit of times past. Why did they exchange the term "catechism" for "catechesis"? What most of the good people do not know is that catechesis means "teaching of the Christian religion by the question-and-answer method." That is exactly what catechism used to do! Anyhow, it was not only a smoke screen. Under the guise of a synonym, it seems now, one wanted to make acceptable things quite different from the catechism of our childhood. Yes, certainly, one continues to teach by the question-and-answer method, but the subject is often broad. The questions themselves are often ridiculous or badly intended. As to the answers, they no longer carry the stamp of eternal verity but of the framework of social-political or other convictions of those responsible for the formation of priests as well as laymen.

The tendency of these so-called catechists is clear: Those in the region of Paris have organized to demand higher salaries and better hiring practices and working conditions, as if they were hourly workers or salespeople in the big shops.

Everywhere, we can see these politically activist "chaplains" and "involved" laymen, forming clubs to do their "catechesis," where one discusses the "question of knowing" if Jesus Christ was, or was not, the Che Guevara of his time, or if the *Little Red Book* of Mao will become the gospel of our times. One could easily put together a dreadful anthology of what is done in certain catecheses. Catholics and even atheists would not recover from their surprise.

J.H.: That is true. I myself undertook some work of that sort three years ago: I didn't know if I was coming or going. I found out that certain chaplains, without consulting the parents, found it all right to impart sex education to their charges, and this evidently made for a big audience.

Those courses, unhappily, were often quite off the track. Lack of competence made these teachers guilty of such nonsense, which, in certain cases, was worse than the whispers circulating among the young during recreational periods.

Another deterrent, likewise very serious, is the total absence of any psychological preparation of these educators, their complete lack of understanding of the state of mind of youngsters reaching the age of puberty. Consequently, they often caused serious damage.

M.L.: Have you seen the Canadian catechism? The chapters have such titles as "Sexuality and Daily Life." The pictures, too, are repugnant. The child who has these texts and pictures before his eyes winds up believing that there is nothing more to life than this.

Christian parents have protested, but unhappily there is nothing they can do. It is enough to look at the last page of the work, which carries the *nihil obstat* from the Commission of Catechesis and the *imprimatur* of Monsignor Gerard-Marie Coderre, head of the Commission for Religious Instruction of Quebec.

But that is not all. Certain catecheses invite the child "to reflect on breaking away." The child is invited to break with everything: with his parents, with tradition, with his links to society, in order to "find himself," in order to get rid of the complexities of society and of the family. The ties with his parents, which are the ties of life, are presented as constraints which bind the child and which must be gotten rid of. This is shocking.

J.H.: Yet, Excellency, those monstrosities do not change the fact that I myself have a horrible memory of the catechism of my youth. Those 500 questions which we had to know by heart! And Grandmother, who always meddled. "What does it mean to lie?" she asked me, for example, before she kissed me, when I went to see her. What punishment! And in the end, what remained with me?

M.L.: A lot!

J.H.: Nothing, I assure you!

M.L.: Could you not answer the question "How many capital sins are there?"

J.H.: That question is too easy, Excellency. There are seven capital sins: pride, avarice, luxury, envy, gluttony and anger.

M.L.: You forgot sloth!
But don't you think that this catechism, once it penetrated your mind, has taken hold of your whole being? So much so that, even subconsciously, you are trying to tame your anger, overcome your envy? Otherwise, how could you explain that the once rebellious young man has become the man you are today? Without doubt, you owe it to the catechism which was hammered into your head.

J.H.: Maybe I owe it also to my own experiences, to my own way of thinking.

Hell

In any case, as you know, it's getting harder and harder to catch a fly with vinegar. Besides, the conditioning I underwent—and you have well characterized it as a conditioning—would not be possible today, because a man now regards himself free and master of himself. Liberty and self-mastery actually produce the true religious spirit.

M.L.: But I fail to understand you at all. To reproach the Church for "conditioning" is like speaking of a mother "conditioning" her child, when she imbues him with ideas which are indispensable for his whole life, for a life in community: propriety, politeness, a taste for work.

I know that you will tell me: "They gave me a complex with this terrible fear of Hell!" But in fact, what you call a complex is nothing but a very laudable reaction of virtue to vice. If this kind of reaction has disappeared today, it is due to the ignorance of what we are and of the goal for which we are striving, Heaven. The forbidden things, which nowadays are called "taboos," seem like road signs which show us the way and help us not to get lost.

In every society which respects itself, the laws are bundles of sanctions. What would a society be without a Ministry of Justice? Thus, to the moral law which helps us to practice the love of God some sanctions are added: Purgatory and Hell.

Today, unfortunately, Hell seems completely forgotten and Cardinal Marty complains that nobody talks any more about the notion of sin. But why has the idea of sin disappeared from the present catechesis? Can one forget that God has established law and punishment? Can one forget that every building consists of pieces which keep it together and that the entire structure would be threatened, if one of these pieces were pulled away?

No more Purgatory, no more Hell, no more Heaven! No more Heaven and Hell makes for no more sin. No more sin means no more prayer, no more sacrifice, no morals. No more morals means no more faithful. Or rather, and herein lies the great danger of the process, faithful who become like orphans in search of another set of morals, another heaven, another religion. This is the reason for the switch of so many Catholics to occult sects, or spiritualism, to charismatics or atheistic materialism, toward a morality which promises to make a god out of man, on condition that "dissenters" be condemned to prefabricated trials, to deportation camps, to summary execution.

DECEPTIVE SCIENCES

Many clerics who were encouraged by the pronouncements of the Council concerning the sciences, that it is necessary to adapt them to the Church, naively believed that they could bend the morals of the Church and adapt them to today's ideas.

One field where moral laws are particularly difficult to enforce, evidently, is chastity. To bring down that barrier meant to court favor with the modern world. That was a genuinely Satanic temptation.

The Evil One told the clergy: The pill, which will eliminate the danger of maternity, will upset all morals. If the Church does not give up her ideas in this matter, she will soon be left behind and abandoned. It is therefore necessary that the Church, too, participate in the liberation of the sexes. And they believed Satan.

Too many priests became involved in tearing down the idea of chastity. The gears start to turn toward sex education courses, to replace the catechism, then to scandalous indulgence toward "experiences" of the young and the selfishness of homes that do not want children. On top of it all the January 1973 issue of the Jesuit journal *Etudes* suggested that parents of an unwanted child could practice abortion.

J.H.: Yes—but the Holy See immediately reacted. *Osservatore Romano* published an article by Cardinal Caffara saying:

"This is one of the clearest indicators of the manner in which a certain theology today bows before the world and prostitutes itself before it, instead of bending the knee only in the presence of Our Lord Jesus Christ, and his authentic word, as it was transmitted by the apostolic succession."

M.L.: Who has sowed the bad seed? It does not help to decry the consequences. Besides, nobody listens to reprimands. The modern theologians, or rather the Modernists, point to the "overture" of Vatican II. And their pernicious theses, accepted everywhere, are presented under the label "Catholic."

But who is today slapped down by a suspension *a divinis*? Is it the one who bows to the world, or the priests of Econe, who kneel only "before our only Lord, Jesus Christ"? Whose side is the Vatican actually on, in spite of its protestations?

But to come back to our topic. In whose name do the Modernist clerics express an opinion in a "scientific" way? Do they want you to believe that the new "techniques" have abolished the old laws? Listen to them: They say an abortion is just a passing moment, not even too disagreeable and without any danger.

Unfortunately, they do not read the writings of the real scientific experts, who have studied the physiological and psychological effects. After examining a great number of cases, they can say today that very few women emerge unscathed from this operation. Even in Japan, where this operation has been long legalized and even recommended, the statistics bear out prolonged, ill-fated side effects.

As for the pill, which was destined to ward off the spectre of abortion by eliminating the risks of conceiving and whose use even some confessors today tolerate, all we have to do is to consult a family physician to measure its physical and psychological ravages.

Here too, after the scientific experts had presented the pill as perfectly safe and innocent, the statistics now show endocrine troubles, palpitations, edema, cancer and many other troubles.

The terrible verdict is already in: It was only a pseudo-science which made many, among them priests and faithful, think that the Church is phasing out, that it is archaic and regressive and that there is need for a new morality.

Actually, nature always takes her revenge, when

one disobeys her laws. And the Church knew this very well when she made them her own. True, faithful consorts, living the way God has always wanted, do not risk such troubles.

But we are listening to the sirens of liberalism, and we no longer dare demand that the Christian control his body—not to speak of love, a word that has become so suspicious that one even hesitates to use it any more.

STIMULATORS OR EDUCATORS?

And what are the results? Catechesis, to name only one, has been abandoned. All the teachers of religion must admit it. But many of them refuse to face the truth: young Catholics follow the catechism less and less, because there is less and less talk of religion, and the little atheists, after maybe having quickly and curiously glanced through it, leave disillusioned.

For our youth have been badly understood. Surely, they always want to test their parents, and society, but what they are hoping for is some solid points of support.

Do you know that in the middle of the happenings of 1968, when many of his colleagues courted disorder, a professor appeared in class in his priestly robes and was applauded by the students, for he inspired respect?

During that same troubled period, one of my seminarians had to take an exam at the Sorbonne. I authorized him to wear civilian clothes, if he thought that the clerical robes would be held against him. But the professors themselves asked him to come dressed in his ecclesiastical habit. He did so, and the students, far from showing disapproval, congratulated him.

Believe me, these are not "troublemakers"—again an insidious word—who look after the adolescents; they are educators who are able to set an example. If it were otherwise, how can you explain that the seminary at Econe, where life consists of studies, prayer and spirituality, could attract so many young vocations?

Example is invaluable and irreplaceable. The Church should set a good example in turning down the temptations of a world growing more diabolic every day because it hides the worst perversions under the mantle of "science."

DIVORCE

J.H.: It is evident that you, Excellency, do not value happiness on this earth. I guess that you condemn the action of Monsignor Bourgeois, the bishop of Autin, who is talked about so much in Catholic circles. Not only is he not opposed to trial marriage, but he wants to permit the couple to receive the sacraments.

I must admit my sympathy for this proposal. For in every divorce there is at least one victim. And this victim is treated by the Church as one who is to blame.

M.L.: I don't doubt that there are tragic and painful situations, but to give the transgressors of the law the advantages of those who observe it means to have no laws at all. What protects marriage is fundamental for the good of society. You have only to look around you to see the great increase in divorces caused by abandoning the law.

Talk to a judge in juvenile court. Where did the greater part of boys and girls who have fallen foul of the law come from but from broken homes? Pushed around from one parent to another, or, even worse, torn by the quarrels of their parents, they are often frustrated, unstable, their lives spoiled. The number of such children is constantly increasing, as the divorce rate is constantly going up.

But why this development? Because divorce has become a "normal" thing, and it will become even more so if, to the new shame of the Church, Monsignor Bourgeois and now also Monsignor Etchegaray are able to prevail.

It is here, as everywhere, that you can see the fatal imprint of the Evil One. From the moment that divorce is no longer under sanction, marriage, which can be cut short without any harm, is no longer important. The engaged person is no longer anxiously concerned with the character of the partner. They can get married on a whim.

All this bodes ill, but it gets even worse. Instead of making an effort to understand each other better, they are like passengers on a boat who, for a while, share a trip and let their quarrels get out of hand and become irreparable.

You will probably object that it is better to go through a divorce, with all its trauma, than continue to live in the silence of hatred. But don't deny that a deep respect might have been born instead of this hate, if both partners, in the light of God, had made an effort to understand each other.

Under the pretext that one must understand the drama of, so far, only a few faithful, the bishop of Autin is involved in an undertaking which will greatly increase the victims of that drama! I hope you will understand now why the eternal Church has proclaimed the indissolubility of marriage, and has punished severely those who transgress that law. Of course, this is infinitely hard on couples who have seen their marriage go on the rocks in spite of all their attempts at coming to an understanding. They deserve the "fraternal" comfort of priests and bishops. But the law is the law; exceptions would soon reduce it to nothing. Don't the bishops see that, between permitting trial marriage and permitting divorced couples to receive the sacraments, a religious marriage has become worthless? And that, sooner or later, a successor will plead in favor of free love?

La Vie Catholique will probably write of such a future bishop what they did about the present one: "Bishop Such and Such has some excellent ideas: More power to him!"

This, now, is where Vatican II has brought us: to hail the courage of a bishop who questions one of the most sacred laws of the Church? It now takes courage to defend the law, in the face of the world's sarcasm and ridicule.

Since we have been talking about the sacrament of marriage, let me express my astonishment over some of the present celebrations. How many engaged couples compose their own parody of a marriage ceremony, puffed up by personal pride, instead of humbly relying on the traditional texts, so full of truth and poetry?

As you know, the fashion is "personalizing." One wants to be "original," to express one's own ideas on the meaning and the end of marriage. They say this is really Christian. But this sometimes leads to ceremonies which are really pagan, as sometimes they resemble a secular, family banquet, with profane singing inside the church.

I can imagine the mother who wants to lead her son to the altar, who will be deprived of this joy. Her son will say to her: "I myself have chosen my wife, not you; therefore it is *I* who will lead *her* to the altar. That is the true Christian spirit." As if Jesus Christ recommended this vainglory, which would deny a mother this walk, so symbolic for the role she had played in the Christian upbringing of her son!

When I am present at certain marriages, I would like to close my ears to the cacophonies of certain songs, and the verbiage of the witnesses—parents and friends of the bridal couple—and to reread a text like the following, which is, of course, never used these days:

"Faithful and chaste, may she marry in Christ and follow the example of holy women. May she be the beloved of her husband, as Rachel was; may she be as wise as Rebecca, and as long of life and faithful as Sarah. May her actions give the Author of Lies no power over her. May she keep strong in the faith and in the Commandments; true to one marriage bed, may she shun unlawful embraces. May she strengthen her weakness by firm discipline, be sedulous in her modesty, honored for her chastity, learned in the truths of Heaven.

"May she be rich in children, may she prove virtuous and blameless, may she come to rest with the blessed in the kingdom of Heaven. And let them both see their children's children to the third and fourth generation and live to a happy old age. May marriage be for her a yoke of love and peace."

This is the entire text. Monsignor Bourgeois should be interested in rereading it.

THE CHARISMATICS

J.H.: We'll never finish reviewing what you call "the bad fruits of the Council." The integrist and traditionalist newspapers and weeklies have used tons and tons of paper and ink to review them and castigate them.

M.L.: Don't you think that those we have mentioned are enough cause for Catholics sometimes to use strong language in defense of their faith, against all those abominations?

J.H.: Above all, what strikes me most personally is the flight of so many faithful toward "others," as they would say today. Many are attracted by religious sects—and the Pentecostals are one of them, it seems. Moon's seductions still tempt many youngsters. And finally we have to talk about the "farthest out" of them all, Monsignor Menie Gregoire and his "radio confessional."

M.L.: I think everything has already been said about this and can be lumped together with what was said about the new catechesis. Far from holding the faithful, the demagogues of the conciliar Church discourage them and make them quit.

The phenomenon of Menie Gregoire, self-appointed counselor of the married life of others, is certainly the most symptomatic. He probably owes his origin to the fact that the Church has let the sacrament of penance fall into disuse, and that it therefore no longer fulfills its function as a guide of conscience.

The success of the Moon sect shows how easily one can deceive the young under the guise of an ideal, even a very austere one. Here again a sect replaces the void left by the absence of the true teachings of the doctrine revealed by Our Lord.

J.H.: But what about the Pentecostals, sometimes also called Charismatics? That is a truly remarkable phenomenon.

Cardinal Suenens, the primate of Belgium, has written a quite extraordinary book about it. The cardinal actually believes that the Catholics who unite to pray by chanting, dancing and expressing themselves without restraint find themselves in the company of the Holy Spirit. The cardinal also firmly believes that these Catholics then start to "speak in tongues," like the apostles on the day of Pentecost; that they may have prophetic visions and heal by the laying on of hands. He writes:

"Some Charismatics express themselves by totally unknown idioms, doubtless of people who have forever vanished and are forgotten."

The view of the primate of Belgium is not unique. A Dominican, for instance, Father Albert de Mauleon, who also has studied the question, shows a similar enthusiasm. In a rather surprising manner, he wrote:

"All they have to do [the Charismatics] is to ask: Spirit, are you here? And he responds by the most improbable feat, to restore the old and most motheaten Christendom!"

In this, the priest joins the cardinal, who, after stating that the Holy Spirit is not a phantom, continues:

"What is so striking about the experiences of the Charismatics is not the novelty, but the resurgence of the original tradition and the rediscovery of our own point of departure."

The Holy Father himself seems convinced, since he received in the Basilica of St. Peter—I think it was last year—more than 10,000 Charismatics, who assured him they represent a million Catholics, 20,000 of them from France.

M.L.: This return, so to say, to the past is nothing but a bad caricature of the past.

That Christianity, in the beginning, needed particular graces, mostly the blood of martyrs, to take hold and expand, that I can well believe. But those graces depended on the reception of the sacraments, and not on a sort of initiation rite which resembles a diabolic rite. Some Charismatic sects need a laying *off* of hands, which means abandonment of self to the Holy Spirit!

This seems to me like a diabolic alienation, for the "Spirit" does not come through the sacraments but by the laying on of hands outside them. This leads to a contempt for the sacraments and also for authority, since the "Spirit" is received outside the Church, outside his sacred ministry and outside the sacraments. One can easily wind up by exchanging faith for hysteria.

THE CASSOCK

J.H.: Now, Excellency, we must talk about today's priests whom Cardinal Marty has defended so brilliantly. I can understand them. Having met a number of clergy and having known them well, I am convinced that the majority of them are saintly men who are pure and courageous and unusually dedicated.

The problem for most of them is that they are between the devil and the deep blue sea, so to speak. On the one hand, they see where these excesses are leading; on the other, they do not want to cut themselves off from the world. The temptations to which they are subjected are numerous and strong. Some of them are terribly troubled and unhappy.

M.L.: Since one was searching for a "new type of priest," as it were, adaptable to the ways of the world, this was to be expected.

Look at the chain of events: The first objective is to obliterate the image of the priest, as he was once recognizable immediately by the cassock. "The priest," they say, "is a man like any other." Once this is recognized as a principle, everything else follows inexorably. For these were the ideas which governed the world: change the ideas and you change the world. The weak and the naive then say: "The world changes and we have to change with it." This is a triumph of perversion.

J.H.: You are talking about giving up the cassock, but these clothes were not adopted so far back. Does one really have to ask priests and religious of 1977 to hamper themselves by what is really, I think, a highly impractical garment?

M.L.: Under certain circumstances, I admit that the cassock is a very impractical garment. On a ship, for instance, or in a high wind; but it has so many advantages that it was really ridiculous to give it up.

Some time ago, when I was a missionary, when I had to walk on foot for entire weeks through the equatorial forests, I had my white robe in my luggage. One day, the bush Africans remarked to me: "Father, you should wear your cassock, for the wild tribes would otherwise take you for a Protestant minister and would be scandalized." Since then, I have always travelled in my cassock, in river boats or on airplanes, and I have noticed that everywhere the priest is greatly esteemed and respected, except in the Anglo-Saxon countries.

Far from being an obstacle, the priestly garment reassures travelling companions and draws out confidences, as I have never failed to observe during my 6,000 hours of flying time all over the world. How many priests would be able to testify, like the priest of a great city who told me:

"Since most of the Catholics who live in the new district have no telephone, and since a highway leads around these quarters, I always make my daily rounds by bicycle, wearing the cassock. The people know this. Those who want me come to their window. They can recognize me far off by the cassock, and they call me."

During an audience on November 22, 1972, Pope Paul VI declared: "The habit does not only identify who wears it but it gives the wearer an internal confidence of what he is supposed to be." How true!

On that occasion, Paul VI commented favorably on a decision by the Sacred Congregation for Religious, which did not make it obligatory to wear the habit but which stated explicitly: "Except for special occasions, priests must wear a gray suit with a Roman collar." Actually, this decision was made to stem the "fashion" which led an ever-increasing number of priests to "laicize" their dress. It was hoped that by proposing a middle way, that is, the habit of the Protestant clergyman, things would fall back in line. Of course, they did nothing of the kind. Since we could throw the cassock to the winds, why not do the same with the gray suit and the Roman collar?

In the month following, the Conference of Bishops of Quebec stated, in contrast to the decision of the Congregation of Religious, and the opinion of the Holy Father: "The documents of the Sacred Congregation of Religious do not concern the clergy of Quebec, who are authorized to wear civilian clothes of their choice."

Those bishops of Quebec: have they been admonished as they deserve? This was not according to the Council spirit. Exchanging the cassock for civilian clothes has now brought us some long-haired priests, dressed in jeans and T-shirts.

At that time I was superior general of the Congregation of the Fathers of the Holy Spirit and I saw where all this would lead to. That is why I addressed a letter to them:

"The wearing of the habit characterizes the religious. It goes without saying that this means a sense of modesty, discretion and poverty. It is evident that this particular garment should call for respect and make people think of detachment from the vanity of the things of the world. . . .

". . .But we have to recognize that the wearing of civilian clothes has made enormous progress in spite of the enactment. . . . It is therefore important to ask ourselves: Is it desirable, yes or no, that the priest be recognized and distinguished by faithful and laymen, or, on the other hand, is it desirable today—to make the apostolate more effective—that the priest does not distinguish himself from the layman?

"We answer this question with the idea of the priest according to Our Lord Jesus Christ and the apostles. St. John said: 'You are not of the world, since my choice has brought you out of the world. . . . And you will be a witness because you have been with me since the beginning.' Our Lord said: 'You will be my witnesses.'

"Everybody can understand this testimony without difficulty: 'Men do not light a candle and put it under a bushel, but upon a candlestick that it may shine to all that are in the house.' So says Matthew.

"The priest's habit fulfills these two requirements in a clear and definite manner. The priest is in the world without being of the world; he distinguishes himself by living there. He is also protected against evil. Says St. John, 'I don't demand that you take them away from the world, but that you shield them from the evil, for they are not of this world, just as I am not of it.'"

I wrote further in that letter:

"The testimony of the word, which for a priest is certainly more important than the testimony of his habit, is made much easier by the clear manifestation of his priesthood, which the wearing of the cassock indicates. Civilian clothes obliterate all distinctions and recognition, and make protection from evil much less effective. This disappearance of testimony by habit clearly appears as a lack of faith in the priesthood, a disdain of the religious sense in your neighbor, and above all a laxity, a lack of courage, in your convictions."

I also wrote:

"We have to recognize that a great many Catholics and also a great many priests no longer have an exact idea about the place of religion in society, and all its activities. Laicism has invaded everything, even our primary schools and the secondary schools for seminarians. The priest who lives in such surroundings has an ever-growing sense of alienation from this society, and thinks he is a witness to a past which is definitely out of focus. His presence is barely tolerated. These, at least, are the impressions many young priests carry away. And so we have this craving to fall in line with the laicized, de-Christianized world, which reveals itself by the abandonment of the habit.

"These priests do not have a clear idea of the place of priests in the world, and in regard to the world. They have not been around much, and they judge these ideas only superficially. If they had spent some time in the less atheistic countries, they would have been edified, finding that faith in the priesthood is still alive and, thank God, very much so in most countries of the world.

"To fall in line with laicism and atheism means to capitulate and remove the last obstacles to their spread.

"The priest is a walking sermon through his habit and his faith. The apparent absence of a visible priest, especially in the great cities, is a great disadvantage to the preaching of the Gospel.

"The priest is the salt of the earth. And St. Matthew says: 'But if the salt loses its strength, what should it be salted with? It is no longer of any use but to be thrown out and trodden under foot by men.' Well, is it not this which is in store for the priests who do not want to appear as such? The world will not love but despise them. The faithful will be sadly affected by not knowing with whom they are dealing. The habit is an authentic guarantee of priesthood."

J.H.: Your Excellency, that was a very courageous letter. Above all, the phrase "The world will not love them for it but despise them" was prophetic. It called forth the invectives which, among others, Maurice

Clavel*—to name only one—hurls against those who first "lifted the seams," then threw away all cassocks. But were the Fathers of the Holy Spirit guided by your exhortations?

M.L.: Some were, some were not. The worm of liberalism was in the apple, and it was late. The antitraditional wind was already blowing. Often seized by the disastrous ideas of the modern world, my colleagues fancied that a religious congregation should become a democratic society. Once more, everything falls in place.

A Revealing Act

J.H.: You are right, Excellency. But there is an old proverb: "The habit does not make the monk." If it is true that the habit is responsible for establishing the identity of the priest in the eyes of the faithful, it would be a very weak character and a frail vocation that depends on this kind of protection. With or without the habit, a good priest is a good priest.

M.L.: Yes—but it is a mistake to believe that character, even a strong one, and a vocation, even a solid one, are without fault. Those who believe themselves best armed against temptations can succumb just as well as others, and often after a struggle which used to be victorious. There is no lack of examples for that. But the habit is a barrier against ambiguous situations in uncertain issues.

---

*Author of *Dieu est Dieu, Nom de Dieu!*

The reason I have dwelt on this topic is the fact that giving up the habit or the cassock is a concrete and visible sign, a symbol for many other things which are given up. All this is done as if certain members of the clergy want to get rid of the habit to prepare the way for other disavowals, in which, unfortunately, they drag a great number of faithful with them.

I might cite here a number of deplorable or scandalous instances, but it is always the same. Wherever one puts down precise places and dates, it is a direct and easily recognizable attack on a person. If facts are reported without dates and places, then one is suspected of calumny.

But, since it is necessary to support one's contentions, an incident of some significance will serve as an example.

In November of 1972, Archbishop Guyot of Toulouse suspended one of his young priests in an important parish. It was a decision which was self-explanatory: this young man lived openly with a young girl and did not show any remorse about it.

The next Sunday, this young priest, and five others who were on duty at the parish, distributed leaflets in which they declared that they were all leaving the parish together. They wrote: "The gesture of the Archbishop reveals the injustice and the oppression by persons who, at the moment, dominate the Church."

Can you imagine such a thing? Yet it happened. Six priests from the same parish, signing this tract insulting the Church of Our Lord Jesus Christ, which they elected to serve of their own free will, knowing well what it was all about, and who had promised to serve according to the rule of the celibate!

And why, after all? Because they wore civilian clothes better to mingle with the people; because, once out in the world, they wanted to submerge themselves in it. They worked in it, they made a living in it.

A good article was published about the time of this incident:

"Instead of administering the sacraments, they worked, and in consequence of living in an environment that is not chaste (why should it be chaste?) they succumbed to temptation. What they should reproach the hierarchy for is that it did nothing to prevent them from giving themselves up to the joys of love, but permitted them to be put into a situation where it became psychologically and physically impossible for them to respect celibacy."

J.H.: Should we blame the bishops?

M.L.: What must be blamed is the spirit of change, the false discovery which questions everything, to such an extent that there is neither conviction nor firmness in one's faith.

In this sense, the bishops, whose task it is to preserve the faith with firmness, have failed in their duty by omission, by cowardice before public opinion.

LETTER OF A DISSATISFIED CATHOLIC

J.H.: But Excellency, some members of the clergy

often have a certain air which does not facilitate the task of the bishops. Some time ago, a friend brought me an issue of *La Croix du Nord Dimanche*, which is, presumably, the voice of the archbishop of Lille. So many readers had apparently written to that paper with complaints that it had been necessary to publish at least one letter. It probably came from a good father of a family, who wrote:

"I am not a pimp nor a prostitute; I am just a Christian who is also rich. Therefore, I am a hypocrite. Does that give me the right to express myself in the columns of your organ?

"I would like to tell you what many see in our parishes.

"If you are a priest and if you wish to see your bishop in order to talk to him, a secretary will tell you that the bishop is very busy and one must not clutter up his appointments unnecessarily.

"But if you urgently want to be laicized, you will be immediately received by the bishop, who will say: 'Fine, fine, my son.'

"If you are a pastor, ridicule devotions to the Blessed Virgin; refuse, with a wink, to bless a rosary; tell the young that they have to liberate themselves and that Mass attendance is no longer obligatory; preach a neo-exegetic theology about the resurrection of Our Savior and you are a participant in the pious work of stripping away from the Church what has been her shame throughout the centuries.

"But if you are a pastor who visits the sick, are in the confessional every day, have the rosary said during the month of Mary and sometimes celebrate a Latin

Mass, you 'smother the spirit of Vatican II.'

"If you are married, if you desire a private baptism, if you send your children to Catholic schools, if you want them to make their profession of faith with their colleagues and not in the parish, you unleash a severe homily. It will liken you to those Christians who have extinguished within themselves the ardor of the Spirit and who hold back the advance of the Church and by this give their blessings to the Marxist revolt.

"Your offer to serve as a lector at Sunday Mass will be refused; the epistle will be read by a young divorcee who has remarried and whose marital happiness gives a glow to the parish. Besides, she is very 'receptive' toward Peter (the pastor).

"If you are 16 years old, if your school work and your scouting activities absorb you and those of class delegate prevent you from going to teach the alphabet to the illiterate, you are already carrying 'all the marks of capitalism.'

"But if at the same age—high school junior—you have a liaison which 'lends a sense to your life,' even if your parents reproach you for it, and if you refuse to pray, in your disappointment, 'that spiritual cancer that is the Sunday Mass,' the vicar will give you his office every Saturday afternoon so that you can make points with your girl friend. He himself, during that time, will go to a nearby coffee house and, with three militant Communists, will prepare his Sunday sermon.

"If you are hesitant about the kiss of peace, if you do not like the cocktail get-togethers after Mass, where the pastor, in light trousers and a red sweater, pats the bottoms of young girls whom one never sees at Mass, you are increasing the 'ranks of those Pharisees at whom Our Lord has turned up his nose.'

"If you die as a lecturer of the Confraternity of St. Vincent de Paul after 40 years of devout attachment, the pastor will refuse to mention this devotion during the funeral sermon, because he considers it a sop which eases the conscience but, in pretending to aid the Church of the poor, hides social injustice.

"But if you are divorced, having left your spouse with two children, and are running around with a divorcee who has three, a priest will exalt your 'family and Christian virtues.'

"If you ask the Church for a pop concert which will reveal to the young people 'the true face of the Church,' you will get permission with good will. The confessionals will even serve as alcoves.

"If you want to celebrate your 50th wedding anniversary with a nephew who is a priest, surrounded by your numerous and outstanding Christian family, and if you ask for this celebration to take place in your own parish, between two Masses, you risk being refused. 'You must understand, sir, that we are to testify that this is the Church of the people of God, not a gathering of clans.'

"I therefore demand of myself: Has Christ ever let his apostles and disciples down? Has he ever ridiculed and scoffed them in order to entertain prostitutes?

"I can put at your disposal all the proof for what I said above, with dates, addresses, witnesses."

We may wonder what made a very "conciliar" newspaper publish such a letter, which is particularly fierce and defiant. The same issue of *La Croix du Nord*, February 15, 1975, also published a very long reply, which meant to combine "humor and compassion." We read:

"That woman who was a remarried divorcee and, as you say, too willing to read the scriptures in public and to visit the ministers in private, reminds me of another, who was married five times and had the sixth husband on trial, and who came to draw water at Jacob's well; we have heard of her from Jesus Christ by way of St. John."

At any rate, that the letter and its reply were published at all is symptomatic of the uneasiness that is admitted even by the bishops, an uneasiness which has been a long time coming. It takes a few years of excess before the faithful start to complain.

That is why a participant of the press conference, called by the bishop of Lille on the eve of your Mass to warn his flock against you, was able to say:

"Your position, Excellency, is quite understandable, but you have to admit that priests in your diocese have committed many errors. But you have never found it useful to call a press conference, as you do now, to point out their errors. Had you done so, maybe the actions of Archbishop Lefebvre, which concern us so much today, may not have found the vindication which they are finding now."

On that day the bishop of Lille, who, among others, accused you and your followers of "intoxication," was tempted to employ a ruse. He said he had received a very imposing amount of mail. That was true. But by singling out one that was hostile to you, he gave the impression that all of them were in the same vein. In fact, a great many faithful had taken advantage of your coming to Lille in order to write him, firmly but with respect, what they thought about certain events in today's Church.

CAPTIVE BISHOPS

Take note, then, the bishop of Lille is greatly respected by the faithful, who appreciate his humility, his radiant goodness, his extraordinary humanity. Even those who criticize him nevertheless sympathize with him. They certainly do not wish to be in his place. They find that, given the circumstances, he is doing his best.

M.L.: It is true, many bishops complain that they are no longer free, that they feel chained down. Yet, if this prevents them from persecuting progressives, they certainly are not prisoners when it comes to finding fault with true priests and true Catholics. Some time ago—that is, until the Vatican Council—a bishop was master of his diocese. He was the direct representative of the Holy Father and thus had the complete confidence of the successor of St. Peter. He could, therefore, act himself or for his superior, according to the needs of Jesus Christ, depending on the territory in which he found himself. It is a pity that the Council introduced that new and pernicious idea of collective government. No bishop can henceforth make a decision by himself. He has to refer to the Conference of Bishops of his country.

This system, of which the skillful strategists can easily grab hold, given the half-heartedness of a great many bishops, favors demagoguery. It hurts and checkmates even the strongest characters and the most enlightened ones, who are already experiencing difficulties in their own dioceses.

You have to recognize all the consequences of the new ideas of church government which originated in and developed directly from Vatican II.

Many of the young curates do not see what the pastors, archpriests and bishops are really good for. They therefore undermine their authority. They apply pressure, so much so that these men sometimes really feel like prisoners. They prevent certain bishops from expressing themselves as they want to, and they carry the weaker ones with them on their way to dereliction. Now, this perversion has an imperceptible, but very concrete, effect on the whole of the Church. Acting like political cells, groups of ecclesiastics have banded together to pack the commissions and assemblies of bishops. The new bishops, therefore, have made their choices from their ranks.

As far as Econe is concerned, the result is distressing. I have reason to believe that several dozen bishops in Western Europe look favorably upon our seminary. But since they represent the minority and are tied to the majority, none of them can say anything. They try hard to let me know in all sorts of ways, by their encouragement and their prayers, indicating at the same time that they cannot do a thing to help me.

J.H.: These lines of communication are unreliable. You may be mistaken about the meaning of the messages that reach you.

M.L.: Sometimes I ask myself . . . But when the concerned parents of one of my seminarians went to a bishop who has publicly condemned me to ask him to which other seminary they should send their son, he replied: "Tell him to stay at Econe, for only there will he get an education worth its name!" I cannot be mistaken about the meaning of that message! I regret that this bishop is obliged, at least for his public acts, to rely on the "collective conscience," rather than his own.

Priests "In Search"

The sorry condition of today's bishops is demonstrated very clearly by the pitiful state of their seminaries, by their weak, if not nonexistent, recruitment for those seminaries, and for the type of teaching which goes on there. In this field, as in others, the Church has come to meet the world. But unfortunately, and this is very serious, its future is at stake.

There are two ways to analyze the crisis of the clergy. The proper way is this: One could have said with good reason that this crisis is simply a consequence of the ideas of Vatican II. Even at the time of Vatican II, however, priests were troubled by manifestations of pseudo-science, the dangerous attractions of the "consumer society," and the false pretenses of liberalism and Marxism. Satan, who had ensnared many of them, so that they followed in the wrong way, made them demand more and more liberties. It was due to a lack of firmness on the part of the Church that it went so far and that priests prepared to claim even more in order to come to terms with the world.

Actually, they had a bad conscience. They knew well that the Church is not here to be a member of but the head of the body. They expected, perhaps subconsciously, that the bishops assembled for Vatican II would redress the balance, would loudly proclaim the eternal truth, would let it be known that the Church would never buckle under, and would exhort the assembled flocks to follow their example.

In this way, they would have galvanized and organized the priests and thus regrouped the Catholic flocks around good and courageous pastors, and this in spite of what the demagogues might have said about it.

Some ecclesiastics, already corrupted, doubtless would have followed; but the Church would have moved away from them, showing that truth is eternal. At the same time, she would have given comfort to the priests and the faithful who were on the right path. Then the seminaries would have been filled again, for many young men in the world, let me stress this, are looking for purity and an ideal. They want to serve God. The vocations which present themselves at Econe, in spite of the serious questions stemming from the hostility of the Vatican, are an indication of this.

But bad shepherds have led the flocks into temptation, rather than away from it.

To flatter the new ideas of the world, one has been given to understand that the truth of Our Lord Jesus Christ is not the only one and, as the world has changed, the expression, the content, and even the nature of the faith should be changed. Thus, the door was open for disputes, interpretations, experiments, and doubt.

To express it differently, one has taken the compass away from the priests and faithful and then they started their search. They disputed, interpreted, experimented, only to lose themselves in the wilderness of doubt.

What can a priest do, who doubts and sees that the Church itself questions herself, except abandon the priesthood?

This is the real tragedy of the conciliar Church, the concrete sign of bankruptcy of hearts and souls. These desertions are becoming more frequent all the time and a matter of course. Some priests leave their ministry, their parish and their faithful with the attitude of an employee who has given an eight-day notice because of an impossible job situation. They explain over the radio and TV networks that they did not feel comfortable there, or they want to explain their cowardice in the name of "moral convenience."

Have they abjured their vows of celibacy to marry? In order not to cause scandal and pain and to show publicly how little the Church cares about tradition, it turns out that their bishop agrees to be the godfather of their first-born!

Many consider themselves "charity cases." They have betrayed the faithful, but they demand that these same faithful find a position "worthy" of them and their wives. Were they not a cadre, responsible for big businesses? (The big parishes often have a membership of 10,000 Catholics.) They need a gross income of 6,000–8,000 francs a month!

Can you imagine what demoralizing effect all this has on those saintly priests who have remained faithful to their vows of chastity and poverty and faithful toward their flock? What a scandal, even in the eyes of atheists!

We must tell you the story of a priest-worker who became the union spokesman for the far left in the shop where he was working. One day, he discovers love and announces that he is going to get married. Those militants in general don't believe in God or the devil, but what do they do? They get the head of the workshop and they tell him: "Only a practicing and respected Catholic like you could make Comrade Priest understand that a priest simply does not do that!"

Even the atheists are very troubled by the delinquency of the conciliar Church.

Unfortunately, the bishops, or in most cases their entourage, were not able to analyze the crisis of the priesthood in this fashion. They believed, and repeated it, that the massive desertion of priests was due to the fact that they had not been sufficiently in contact with the world, its appetites, its temptations and its truths. Instead of alleviating the crisis of the priesthood, they have only aggravated it.

GFU AND GFO*

The bishops have transformed their seminaries into "search groups" and "formation groups," oriented to academic and workmen circles: the GFU's and the GFO's. These are "sit-down seminaries," where it is no longer a question of a vocation but of a "ministerial project." And who are the young people who form the GFU's and the GFO's?

J.H.: The bishops in general and Cardinal Marty have many good things to say about them.

M.L.: How can they criticize what they themselves wanted, or at least accepted for the sake of peace and quiet?

Actually, many others have a different opinion. The way these groups are conceived, the "search groups" attract those who are "seeking," rather than those who want to enrich, fortify and deepen their faith and their vocation. They often attract those young people who want to make the world over, or especially Catholicism, for, according to them, Jesus Christ is the "permanent revolution."

They therefore question everything, even the bishops, though they, I imagine, want nothing but their good. But for some among them, the bishops are comparable to the PFG,† which the Catholic collec-

---

* Groupe Formation Universitaire and Groupe Forunckon Oeuvrière.

† PFG is a French equivalent of a supervisory council.

tivism would like to relegate to the attic. Is it necessary to state that the majority of the GFU and GFO are highly politicized and unionized—on which side it is easy to guess. Some of them live in boarding houses where there also are young girls and where the sudden interruption of a "ministerial project" is due to a liaison or to marriage. But one should congratulate oneself, because some of those "modern seminarians" ask themselves if God exists and if it would not be necessary "to rethink Catholicism" from A to Z, combining it with other religions and with the invaluable support of Marxism!

It is true that the professors of these young people often impart scandalous teachings. I have before me a lecture given by the chairman of the Department of Theology at Strasbourg. This lecture is heretical from beginning to end. There is no longer even a question about the real presence of Our Lord for the chairman of the Department of Theology in Strasbourg. For him, Our Lord is present in the Eucharist "like a composer who has been dead a long time is present when his music is performed." According to him, there will be no more eucharistic celebrations in a few years. Groups of Christians will get together, without even bread and wine, and will create the feeling of communion with Christ, thus creating a "Eucharist for our times."

At Fribourg the seminarians, mine among them while still there, had to follow the instructions of Father Pfuertner. This Dominican professor of moral theology stated that premarital relations are "normal and desirable." In the same seminary, Father Baumgartner, another Dominican, taught the composition of new canons for the Mass.

These are the seminaries in which the bishops take so much pride and in the name of which they condemn our seminary at Econe, a school where there are serious vocations and which is always faithful to the Church.

In addition, the bishops assert that their "search groups" attract a great number of young people—in reality, hardly twenty a year, in the big dioceses. They forget to mention that many of these young people, after two or three years, continue their "search" in a different direction, their "ministerial project" having completely evaporated.

Is it really the Church's purpose to start forming two kinds of priests, "academics" and "workingmen," as if the Church had already adopted the clearly defined collective schemas?

There is nothing to be surprised about in any case: many new priests come from these "search groups" and consequently they have an absolutely insufficient religious formation. Many swim in the stream of a collectivist utopia. With Abbot Fumonier, another one of their professors, they are telling us that "our generation can finally write a fifth gospel, a gospel according to our times"!

What a program! We can therefore expect that the clergy of tomorrow will consign the Gospels according to Matthew, Mark, Luke and John to the ash can so they can set up another, "the one for our own times." This is when "St. Marx" and the extreme leftists will prove to us that they are the right interpreters of the

Bible and the only true apostles of Jesus Christ.
But they are not censured by the Vatican.

MIDNIGHT MASS WITH SLIDES

J.H.: This fifth gospel might come from a text which actually is steeped in Christianity, the "Declaration on Human Rights."

This is the way the Discalced Carmelites must understand it, because the main reading at their midnight Mass at Christmas in 1975 was this "Declaration on Human Rights," which was chanted, like a Greek chorus, by several voices. Please note—good republican and democrat that I am, a good citizen, devoted to the "Declaration on Human Rights"—that I prefer, especially at the Carmelites, to hear "Peace on Earth to Men of Good Will," which says even more in one beautiful phrase.

But you should know that there are even more surprising "midnight masses." Father Lelong, a Dominican, told about a Mass in the Church of St. Germain-de-Vitry-sur-Seine on December 25, 1974:

"The Mass began quite normally. But after the *Christ have mercy*, the assembly was asked to look at slides on three screens mounted above the altar.

"About forty slides flashed on and off. First there were some very peaceful landscapes, followed by less peaceful ones (postmen on strike, union banners, abandoned houses, war in Vietnam), all this in contrast to banquet scenes in rich middle-class houses in the midst of luxury.

"The show was accompanied by extracts from the Song of Songs, and a couple in each other's arms dallied a while on the screen. There was also a shot of high ecclesiastical dignitaries in full ceremonial robes with the caption 'Prelates Relaxing.'"

This is a terrible aberration, especially in view of the beauty of the Christmas midnight Mass, which is so moving, so vibrant and filled with so much hope! We could go on quoting similar cases forever.

Father Bruckberger, he too a Dominican but not of the same ilk, has gotten together a collection of such goings-on in his column in *L'Aurore* in which he speaks freely, to the displeasure of the bishops and especially Cardinal Marty. But it did not do him any good. His order has severely reprimanded him.

M.L.: Poor Father Bruckberger! He might have said whatever he wanted, and even maligned the hierarchy, by appealing to the Council. Nothing bad would have happened to him, since so many others do it and they are never punished.

But proclaiming the truth according to tradition, this—yes, this is schismatic, heretical, and an unpardonable crime!

THE COMMUNION CHANTS

J.H.: As far as I am concerned, I still find, in my visits to many different churches, those where the service is dignified and full of the sense of the holy. But it did happen that I often found tensions, bad taste and obvious foolishness in some of the chants and the liturgies that were being conducted. Thousands of Catholics have already spoken about it, so I won't. But I do want to say that I am really shocked by certain communion hymns. When I was younger, we prayed.

"In the silence of the morning, O Jesus, descend into my soul. Be my companion on the way; my heart ardently calls you." This was probably not a product of genius, but at least it was not vulgar. It was somewhat poetic and was sung to pure and even heavenly music, which invited us to a certain mysticism.

But now, Communion is sometimes gulped like a meal whose only course is the Body of Jesus Christ. I have the horrible impression that I am at breakfast with cannibals, under false pretenses. I had this impression especially one day when the celebrant had the people chant, accompanied by a sprightly music and stomping of feet and clapping of hands: "I have eaten your Body, I have drunk your Blood, Alleluia!"

And what about that communion hymn which made me think of a family barbecue? "He offers us his body like a smell of thyme, and I eat his body like a raisin."

I know, Excellency, that some of these things must shock you. How are we going to get rid of such ideas as these, practiced during some eucharistic celebrations?

St. Marcel I

Yesterday we had lunch with the seminarians at Econe. A frugal lunch, as always at Econe, and, as always, in silence until dessert, but made delightful from beginning to end by the pleasant reading of some pious literature, by one of the seminarians as a chant.

I say pleasant because the reading, which I expected to bore me to death, interested me greatly. It was part of a description by a Pope who had decided to drop the music in the churches and "reduce Church songs to the discipline of plain chant."

Here was a remarkable coincidence! What I was listening to, at your side, was a lecture by Pope Marcel II, who was Sovereign Pontiff at the end of the Middle Ages. His seriousness made me think of one of his predecessors, Marcel I, also a Pope but at the dawn of the Christian era, and who was never duplicitous about his faith: he became a martyr and was thrown to the wild beasts.

Of course, I do not believe that the personality of an individual can depend on his first name. But I do suppose that your parents, whose piety was well known, did not give you the name Marcel only because it sounded good! And I am sure that you studied the lives of these Marcels. I was struck that, on the last page of your work *A Bishop Speaks*, it was indicated that the book was finished "on the feast of St. Marcel I." This cannot be pure coincidence.

M.L.: It is only natural that I should be attached to my patron saint. I pray to him and I try to follow his example.

Plain Chant

We priests really should read again the teachings of Benedict XIV, from which we also read during the meal of which you were speaking. Benedict XIV, who was Pope from 1740 to 1758, said:

"The fantasies of modern music appear contemptible, compared to the harmonies of plain chant and pure psalmody when the latter are done according to the rules.

"This is the reason why today's faithful leave the college and parish churches and run to those of the monks who make piety a rule in their divine services, singing the psalms in holy fashion and with moderation, serving the Lord as the Lord should be served—with great reverence."

As you can see, as early as the eighteenth century priests turned away from sacred chant, probably because of the wishes of the people, but they were wrong. As Benedict XIV notes: the "faithful people," far from being seduced, did not hesitate to show preference to the monks who psalmodized in a holy fashion, as it is done by the seminarians of Econe when they are assembled in chapel, as you were able to see for yourself.

Thank God, many Catholics, though they at first hailed the introduction of questionable hymns in the churches, now brand them as vain and dangerous. Wherever they can, they invariably turn again to the truly sacred chant.

The fruits of the Council are really like an obnoxious juice which turns out to be disgusting, even to those who, a while ago, found it most delectable.

The renewal of Gregorian Chant is a symptom of this. The fact that Cardinal Marty had the Gregorian Mass, which the deceased President Pompidou had wished for his funeral, sabotaged does not change anything in this regard.

The Sense of the Sacred Has Been Lost

Again we have to state: everything—everything remains the same. Why do we have to have in the churches, and up to the moment of Holy Communion, hymns and chants like the one of which you have spoken here? Because the Council, in order to join the Protestants, has dismantled the Mass. It is no longer the summit, infinitely mysterious and holy, the supreme sacrifice which gives us the real presence of Our Lord Jesus Christ, under the guise of bread and wine. It has become a ceremony "recalling" the Last Supper, presided over by a minister of the cult. The Vatican, of course, pretends that there is nothing to it. But how can one explain so many liturgies that seem constructed for the needs of the moment? They are farther away from the true sacrifice of the Mass than the most advanced Protestant commemorations.

Even if the Vatican did not want this, the fact remains that, by eroding the rite fixed forever by the Council of Trent, it has started an imbroglio which even the hierarchy can no longer master. The French bishops, willy-nilly, have come to admit it.

They say: "We shall put on the brakes, force a standstill." But can they cleanse the spirits from the obnoxious germs, by now well developed, to which these spirits have become accustomed? Can they still force a standstill on the young priests who have been brought up in the way we have seen, at the moment when these bishops themselves, by promoting or accepting collegiality, have lost the essential ingredient of their authority, if not their credibility?

Thus, once the Holy Mass is disrupted, the infinite respect which it called forth has evaporated: the sense of the sacred, even the sense of harmony, has been lost.

Everything is now happening in the Church as it does in classes where the teacher has fallen into disrepute. He can admonish and punish as much as he wants; the more he storms, the more excited the students get and the more they lose touch with the competition.

LATIN

J.H.: But Excellency, you have to face things! For myself and also for many of your own followers, the "tinkering" with the Mass that Vatican II has done is well justified. The altar, turned toward the faithful, makes them participate more in the sacrifice. This seems to be a development to which all Catholics by now are accustomed, even gratefully so. How could we possibly return to the past?

Communion in the hand, furthermore, which

shocks you so much and which you even think sacrilegious, should not cause so many difficulties whenever it does not go against the sense of the sacred. If the Council and the bishops, for instance, would have maintained the obligation to fast, if they would have retained the strict notion of sin and the clear obligation to be in the state of grace when receiving Communion, the idea of Communion in the hand might have appeared, even to the traditionalists, as a means of facilitating the administration of the sacrament, without altering the essential mystery of the real presence. I personally like the kiss of peace as it is given in some parishes. Isn't this an eminently Christian process? And as to the use of the vernacular in the liturgy . . .

M.L.: I have already told you I am not at all against the introduction of the vernacular in the liturgy, for the Epistle and the Gospel, maybe, but only if there is a very good translation.

I think the thought of the Church, according to the Council of Trent and the declarations of the Supreme Pontiffs, is that the Latin should be retained from the Offertory to the Communion of the priest inclusively. That would be a minimum. This is the only way to safeguard the truth and unity of the sacrifice and so safeguard the Church. Why? So that Catholics the world over feel they are closely united by this divine sacrifice. And so that there is no opportunity for changes or variations.

Now, the use of vernacular language at this sublime moment of the sacrifice occasions all sorts of translations and, it has to be said, lucubrations which make a good many Masses invalid, even sacrilegious.

J.H.: It is true that in a certain parish the beautiful words of the traditional canon: *Domine, diesque nostros in Tua pace disponas*, have turned into something like: Lord, grant that our souls may move around like a motor with well-oiled pistons!

When we know that in Africa, for example, there are hundreds of vernacular languages, and when we know the pressure exerted by tribal customs, we can imagine where this would lead! We can see that the loss of Latin, which allowed all people and tribes to communicate in the same faith, was a great loss indeed. By striking at the Latin, one struck at the cement which holds together the edifice of the Church. Thus it is a loss for everybody. I heard that the president of Senegal, who a few years ago was received by the Pope in audience, sent him a petition in which he wrote: "I implore Your Holiness to save the Latin, treasure of humanity."

M.L.: It is wrong to say that the Latin prevented the faithful from understanding. The missals provided a line by line translation on the opposite page, in the national language in a clear translation which could be understood by everyone. By contrast, many of our French prayers today are a gibberish which nobody understands, except those who are "initiates," texts which don't belong together. Can one pray under such conditions?

To say that the Mass had to be "adapted" to the faithful is the worst sin of pride. A simple peasant can easily follow the Mass of St. Pius V; how much more a high school graduate.

It is in the communion of all men in the same rite, no matter what their degree of intelligence or their social origins, in which the unity of the Church of Our Lord Jesus Christ is shown forth most brilliantly. I recommend to you a passage from the book *Des moines et des hommes* by Ghislain Lafont. This religious is not at all opposed to the use of the vernacular in the liturgy. Yet he writes:

"Since we have our liturgy in French, I am never moved by preaching during Mass and it never strikes me as being an invitation to prayer. Before that, I was always carried away by the sermons because the Latin ones always had a literary and spiritual quality which exists exclusively in Latin.

"I am thinking especially of the Christmas hymn 'Christe Redemptor Omnium.' It has heavenly music, and is angelic in its simplicity, but it is never sung!"

"THE MASS HAS TO BE DESTROYED"

I can now answer your questions concerning the Mass celebrated facing the faithful and Communion in the hand. You have your reasons. Mine go farther. You certainly will remember that Luther said, speaking of his strategy against Rome: "To strike at the heart of the Church, one would have to demolish the Mass." Yet, in order to obtain his ends, he had to retain certain elements of the old Mass in order not to arouse scandal by changes that were too abrupt.

The enemies of the Church, encouraged by Vatican II, have acted precisely in this manner.

Some of these arrangements are actually necessary. But these arrangements cannot and must not be called into play unless it is a case of hardship. They must not change what we consider eternal. It is necessary for them, in any case, to be clearly defined and fixed by an unimpeachable and uncontested authority, making certain that everything will be kept in line.

But can the conciliar Church assemble these conditions? Absolutely not, as everyone knows. You know it yourself, since you told me that in one parish Communion was given in the form of a roll with raisins. This made one of the children say: "Goody, goody! We shall have a chocolate egg at Easter!"

Isn't that awful? In a certain sense, it is what you would expect. It fits perfectly into the Vatican II logic of changing even the most sacred things.

In the face of this sacrilegious desacralization of the Mass, our beautiful treasure, there is only one thing we can do: uphold tradition. Another admonition that has lost its value.

If one wants to find the roots of the crisis which is shaking the faithful, the clergy, the Church altogether, and whose extent the bishops belatedly recognize, we have only to come back to Luther's analysis: The Holy Mass is the epicenter, the base, the rock of the Catholic Church and of all Catholics. But she is what she always has been, and the pastors and the faithful people find in the divine sacrifice of the Mass, and in the real presence, the unique source which gives them the strength and the courage to be united in faith, in the face of worldly temptations.

To alter it does what Luther has done—makes it a memorial, or even a commemorative assembly, to which everybody gives the meaning that he wants, depending on his own beliefs and inclinations, and thus becomes an object of doubt, the forerunner of atheism.

That is what we have come to. It is not only my opinion but also that of many people, many of whom, since they are not Catholic, can judge more objectively than the Catholics themselves.

GOD IS GOD

J.H.: True, your Excellency, there is no lack of witnesses to the crisis of the Church. Madame Françoise Giroud writes in *Si Je Mente*: "The Church is no longer a refuge for internal solitude; she only adds to the outside confusion." Robert Sole, in *Monde*, December 13, 1972, says:

"Certain chaplains in our high schools always try to be ahead of their times. Some of them, ruined internally, try to project their own disbelief into their teachings."

Maybe M. Sole has read in the *Le Lien*, a quarterly of the National Secretariat of Religious Teachers in Public Instruction, this heartbreaking confession: "Everything is topsy-turvy: my mental categories, which were forged in the seminary—and a post-conciliary one to boot—my faith, my equilibrium, everything is in disorder. Follies and weaknesses, living in insecurity, all this forces us to give up science and wisdom. We are stammering in company with others who stammer."

M. Jacques Sedat, a psychoanalyst, writes in *Autrement* in February 1975:

"It seems that certain priests of today, when they say 'Christ, Christ, Christ,' mean 'I, me, myself.' "

The title of M. Maurice Clavel's book, *Dieu est Dieu, Nom de Dieu!** is quite irregular but it expresses exactly what he wants to say. Some passages are worth quoting:

"My dear Fathers, you have not gone to meet the world; you have surrendered to the world! The bad luck, for you, my dear Fathers, and therefore for us, is that you did not remain in your churches to pray. It means that you have not fulfilled your duty and, after the fact, you are now looking for reasonable excuses. Renegades are not those who lose God but those who exploit and empty Him, and send a curse on those who respect and guard Him. The renegades have a simple and effective means for saving themselves: They condemn those who are faithful! Think of that!"

M. Pierre Chaunu, professor at the Sorbonne in Paris, writes in his book *De l'histoire a la Prospective*: "The intellectual and spiritual mediocrity of the cadres of the Church of the '70s is appalling. An important part of the French clergy today represents a social, intellectual, moral, and spiritual sub-proletariat. . . .

---

* Freely translated, "God is God, Damn It!"

Of the traditions of the Church, this group has not conserved anything but the clericalism, intolerance and fanaticism. These men reject a heritage which destroys them, because they are intellectually incapable of understanding and spiritually incapable of living."

It may happen that the activist revolution will end logically: the process will grind to a halt when there is nothing left to deny. I am sure, Excellency, that you are in agreement with these severe criticisms?

M.L.: Of course. The bishops who assembled at Lourdes were rather uneasy about this appraisal. They would like to arrest this process of the degradation of the Church, before there is nothing more to repudiate.

But while they are waiting they repudiate Econe, where nothing of the eternal Church has ever been repudiated or ever will be repudiated.

7

Providence and the Seminary at Ecône

The First Years

J.H.: And so, judging the Council by its fruits, you wanted to found a seminary with your own means, one that, if I may say so, would be "anticonciliar," in order to maintain "solid doctrine"?

M.L.: I did not want anything of the kind!

I found myself in Rome, where I had just resigned as superior general of the Congregation of the Fathers of the Holy Spirit. They, too, had been infected by the virus of collegiality. They had called a special chapter which was to turn everything upside down. They needed "a direction-giving team," commissions, and, of course, debates, lobbies, negotiations, votes, etc.

And these were the same men who, only a few years before, had implored me to take the head post. But I did not want to preside over the ruin of our own congregation, where I had spent so many years. I left them to their "collegiality."

I had a very small pension which barely permitted me to live, but I did not care; I welcomed that retreat which permitted me to pray and work.

It was then that many young people, either recommended or led to me by saintly priests or laymen, began to seek me out. Those young men felt a vocation, felt they were destined to the priesthood, but they found it impossible to prepare for the priesthood in one of the "new" seminaries. They were young people of very high calibre. They did not only seek advice; they also sought spiritual direction. They hoped that I would accept them.

What was I to do? Did I have the right to disappoint them? I always was of the opinion that one has to accept the things the way God sends. I told them:

"I did not call you here. I don't even know you. You came on your own, by your own free will. If you really want to, you will follow a very serious and profound course of studies, you will have a life of prayer and sacrifice, which will sustain your vocation and will permit you, I hope, later to attain a fruitful apostolate."

I am still saying the same things to the young men who feel that they were chosen by Our Lord Jesus Christ, and who come to see me. I have never "called" anybody. I have never held anybody back. God is the master of souls, especially those of future priests. If he sends them to me, all I do is try to point out the right way.

I have them first study in Rome. Unfortunately, it was difficult to get all these young men together and to find the financial wherewithal. There was, of course, the French Seminary, but there I met many difficulties.

I talked to Bishop Charriere, bishop of Lausanne, Geneva and Fribourg. I knew him well: he had come to Senegal in May of 1958 to bless the new church of Fatick, built partly from contributions from his diocese. It was certainly providential that Bishop Charriere should remember his visit to Dakar and the Senegal. He suggested that I assemble my young seminarians at the Catholic University of Fribourg. That is how the "zealots" were founded and later the

International Confraternity of Priests of St. Pius X, for which Bishop Charriere was good enough to sign the founding documents.

But unfortunately, though I had thought that I would find in a university of such standing and repute excellent Catholic teachings, I regretfully had to state the contrary. This university, like the others, had been contaminated by the new ideas. Future priests went there, their hair long and their pants in tatters. And the professors of moral theology held views, as I told you, that were contrary to orthodoxy. My seminarians were quite upset about it. It was not in order to receive that kind of teaching that they had turned to me!

HOW ECONE CAME INTO BEING

Thanks to the good will of some fine Catholics of Valais, I placed my first-year seminarians in a house which they had bought in Econe. I decided, with their permission, to add on to it and make it a true seminary with professors who would be able to form true priests, according to tradition.

J.H.: You enlarged an old house and put up a new modern building, flanked by other buildings. The entire structure would accommodate, in individual rooms, 140 professors and seminarians, and would contain a chapel, refectory, class and study rooms, kitchens, common rooms, and a religious community which took over the services. That must have cost a small fortune!

Where did the money come from? Where is it still coming from? Because now you have other houses: in Germany, in Italy, in England, in the U.S.A., without counting the priories which you just bought to permit the priests whom you ordained to fulfill their ministry.

M.L.: I thank Providence and the intercession of St. Joseph. It was with us as it was with the Little Sisters of the Poor. And, as with them, neither Providence nor St. Joseph has ever abandoned us.

Hadn't I already built, in Senegal, churches, schools, welfare centers, youth hostels? Providence has always helped me and never let my hands be empty.

J.H.: But Excellency, we are talking here about enormous sums! People talk about billions of old francs, of very rich Americans who built "a bridge of gold" for you, of European capitalists who subsidized you.

M.L.: That's completely untrue, pure imagination. People talk without rhyme or reason. As you know, the old house at Econe, with its little chapel, belonged to the Canons of the Great St. Bernard. The canons wanted to sell the house. The buyer wanted to transform it into a hotel, and possibly a hotel of doubtful character. Catholics of the village and of the district were so upset about it that they formed a group to buy it themselves, so that it could remain a house of faith. And we have come to an agreement with them concerning its use.

When I wanted to add on to the house, to make it bigger, I asked myself: "Where will I find so much money?" But confident in St. Joseph, I had great hopes.

At that time, I was about to leave Paris for Rome. A lady called me: she wanted to see me right away. You see, the number of people who want to see me is important. In most cases, it means considerable loss of time. So I tried to avoid seeing that lady. But she was so anxious to meet me, if only for a few moments, that I gave in. She meant to tell me how pleased she was with what I had said at the Council and to promise that she would help me in the battle I was fighting—and that she did most generously.

The new buildings at Econe will be paid for! Always Providence. Providence is here every day and appears in the thousands of Catholics who help us, penny by penny. Actually, big gifts appear and the growing work makes for growing expenses. It is all right to buy old properties but often you have to spend more to salvage them than if you buy new houses! But it is the small gifts of the modest, even poor Catholics that count, and it is thanks to these contributions that we are living. They make it possible for the penniless seminarians to continue their studies. Whatever people say, the majority of our seminarians come from modest, even very modest, backgrounds. Their families cannot afford the cost of room and board, which amounts to 30 francs a day, 28,000 old francs a month.

Thus, millions of Catholics—children that save five francs from their allowance, the households of small pensioners who send us ten francs per month—all make it possible that about fifty vocations can blossom at Econe. Providence!

THE CHAUFFEURS OF THE BISHOP

J.H.: Providence, I am told, also takes care of transportation. Everybody at Econe and roundabout knows the "chauffeurs of the Bishop." There are four of them. They are men from the country, neither rich nor poor, who are completely devoted to you. A phone call, and one of the four is here—to take you to Italy, France or Germany, ready to deliver your reply to the Pope, to the Vatican, ready to drive one of the priests of Econe to one of the priories. Quick, reliable and, above all, often free transportation. When you went to Canada, one of them went with you all the way.

M.L.: True, Providence has willed that there would be such faithful. And for Econe, it is a blessing from Heaven. Thanks to them, I can travel thousands of kilometers, without getting too tired, without having to trouble myself with trains, flights, taxis. This system has another advantage: by often changing my means of transport, I can elude the journalists easier. But what is inconvenient are the conclusions certain people are drawing. They think we have unlimited wealth. Didn't I get to Lille in a "sumptuous white Mercedes" and to the Vatican a few days later in a "prestigious blue S.D.S."? Well, after having driven myself for 47 years, I don't even have a car anymore.

J.H.: The attitude of your seminarians strikes me, Excellency, as having a certain family-like background. This seems to contrast with the fact that half of them are unable to assume the expenses of their studies.

M.L.: That is the grace which shines in their faces and also the custom of wearing the cassock. When they arrive in their civilian clothes, it is easy to recognize the sons of the middle classes and those of working classes. But as soon as they wear the habit, they all have the same appearance. The seminary quickly takes care of all social differences. They are all brothers. It is nothing like when the GFU and GFO get together.

J.H.: In general, it seems to me they are no longer very young men.

M.L.: Some of them enter at seventeen or eighteen years, some of them later. God calls them in his own time. But I am happy with the average age, which is about twenty-three. These are young men who have already finished their studies and sometimes they are very highly educated; they come from great schools, have master's degrees, even doctorates. They have thought deeply and they know what they want.

J.H.: But the life at Econe really is not very attractive. Here is a schedule:

6:00 Rising
6:30 Prime
6:45 Prayer
7:15 Community Mass (first-class and second-class feast days, High Mass is sung at 7:00 a.m., as well as on First Fridays and First Saturdays)
8:00 Breakfast
9:00 Class
10:00 Class
12:15 Sext
12:30 Meal
13:00–14:00 Recreation (Wednesday afternoon, free from 13:00–17:30)
14:15 Class or study
15:10 Class or study
16:00–16:15 Snack
16:15–18:30 Study
18:30 Spiritual lecture
19:00 Community prayer (Rosary, Way of the Cross, etc.)
19:30 Meal
20:00–20:45 Recreation
20:45 Compline and the "grand silence"
22:00 Lights out

That's a very hard life, Excellency!

M.L.: That was the kind of life led in all the seminaries fifteen or twenty years ago. It seems hard at the beginning, but one gets accustomed quickly and time passes incredibly fast.

Should this house not be a house of formation for regularity and silence, for the mastery of self, and all the natural virtues which are the necessary complement to supernatural virtues? But it does not mean that the life is sad. On the contrary. As you saw yourself, all these young men look happy. They have fun.

Last April Fool's Day, they played a little joke on me. The main course for lunch was in a small bowl, with a tight lid. When I lifted the lid, I found clear water with two little fish in it.

J.H.: The enemies of Econe—and God knows there are many—say that the course of study is mediocre, for the simple reason that "no intelligent Catholic can follow you" and that thus the level of your professors leaves much to be desired.

M.L.: People say so many things! For instance, after a visit of inspection in the name of the Vatican here at Econe, Monsignor Descamps, honorary president of the Catholic University of Louvain and secretary of the Episcopal Biblical Commission, declared in an interview with *La Libre Belgique* that we were of "incredible fanaticism."

But he was unable to justify this accusation. Speaking of Econe he said: "The style of this seminary was absolutely in line with tradition and in this sense it was an edifying seminary, with a very sympathetic community, with much order and discipline, a great sense of silence and religious exercises, great faithfulness to all the rules of seminaries such as we have known them." If this is "fanaticism," we must change the definition of the word in the dictionaries. As to the level of our professors, I can vouch that it is altogether excellent, even remarkable.

The superior of the seminary and director of studies is Canon Berthod, who has a Ph.D. in theology. Before coming here he was head of the famous Catholic College at Champitet, and has been superior of the novitiate of the Great St. Bernard order. Among the young chair holders, one comes from Central, another has a master's degree in biology, another a master's degree in history from the Sorbonne. Among the other professors or lecturers, one holds an important chair in a great French Catholic university and is an official member of the household of several dioceses.

Pastoral formation is guaranteed by priests who have had much experience with parish work. Canon law is taught by a great Roman specialist, author of several first-class works. I can therefore say very firmly that the training dispensed here is at least equal in every respect to that in other seminaries. The study lasts six years—as long as medical studies. It does not leave untouched anything a priest should know for his own sanctification, as well as for the happy accomplishment of his ministry among the faithful, in the parish or elsewhere.

J.H.: But, Excellency, what will become of these young priests, since all the dioceses obstinately refuse them? Sometimes, I have to admit, even very nastily. Two of your seminarians told me that, when they were on vacation with their parents, they wanted to visit their respective parish priests and that these two pastors closed the door in their faces! Seems that the sight of a cassock alone was insufferable for them. One observation, though: the same seminarians were easily comforted by the fact that, for example, in the bus which they boarded, many people stood up and said: "Please, sit down." They gave their seats to them and greeted them as priests.

M.L.: Yes, well, at the moment, it is true, the dioceses and the bishops refuse these young priests. But the faithful call them. That is why I have no worries in this regard. Our priests will live by two and three in our priories. They will be able to fulfill their apostolate from there. Those who are already installed there are beloved and respected and have many faithful who watch over them.

J.H.: But what about the worldly temptations which they were spared so far? How will they face them? And how can they advise the adolescents and Catholic couples?

M.L.: I was waiting for that question! Our seminarians each year have three months of vacation. They have ample leisure with their families or in the youth camps which they take care of, or otherwise, to be confronted by temptation. But be assured that our seminarians receive all the instruction necessary about problems of morals.

The advice to the young and to Catholic couples has two sides, a technical one, so to say, and a religious one. The first one is not our concern but that of laymen: physicians, professors, parents of good will who have received the necessary educational preparation. It is different with the moral and religious aspect, which is the priest's concern. Is it necessary to be married, as some pretend, to be able to give counsel and guidance in this field? That means that a physician would be looked upon askance, treating a diabetic, if he never had been a diabetic himself! It is precisely because the seminarians at Econe, and the priests we have formed, have their bodies under control, thanks to a life of work, prayer and asceticism, and thanks also to their courage and their faith. They have credibility in the eyes of Christians who are troubled about a perverted world. The example they are giving enables them to exhort single or married Catholics to obey the law of the Church. Their own experience of chastity allows them to do spiritual counselling.

May it please Heaven that the seminarians who "are questing" in the conciliar Church be of the same calibre!

8

The Savage Condemnation

THE APOSTOLIC VISITORS

J.H.: Your Excellency, I do not want to enter into all the details of your difficulties with the Holy See, which seem to come without interruption. Church historians in a later age will have the task of making an objective and complete analysis.

In the meantime, the majority of Catholics do not understand the ins and outs of this affair. Let us then state them.

I personally am very disturbed by the infinitely painful atmosphere of the process. Often the impression remains that we are dealing with personal opposition, and that there is no lack of blows below the belt, poisonous statements and lies. It makes one think of a tempest in a teapot.

When your troubles began in 1974, your traditionalist seminary had just accepted a considerable number of young men, at a time when the other seminaries, charged with the formation of "new priests for a new Church," began to empty themselves. Besides, money began to flow into your coffers, while many faithful, shocked by the development of the clergy, stopped their contributions to the Church. Was it not necessary to nip that competition in the bud?

M.L.: Churchmen, after all, are only men, and it happens, too, that they are motivated by feelings such as you just described.

The messengers of the Vatican and other "conciliar"

ecclesiastics who have visited us are often astonished by our great success.

They might also experience bitterness and envy. But I do not state such an obvious explanation for the reasons of my difficulty with the Holy See. It is quite possible that these difficulties are now sharpened by personal differences. But they originate as far back as Vatican II. I understood this perfectly when Rome, in November, 1974, dispatched two "apostolic visitors" to Econe to inspect the seminary. They were Monsignor Descamps, whom we already mentioned, and Monsignor Oncelin, a canon law specialist. They reported back unbelievable criticism.

For instance, when they interviewed the young priests about the subject of marriage for priests, the idea of truth, and the Resurrection of Our Lord Jesus Christ, the former put forth scandalous propositions regarding dogma and doctrine.

They stated that one would inevitably come to the ordination of married priests, that the Church was not the only holder of the truth and that the Resurrection of Our Lord was not a certainty.

I was highly indignant to think that it was from Rome that these scandalous declarations reached us. Under the pressure of my indignation, I wrote, on November 21, that famous "declaration" which, to use a popular phrase, really stung to the quick. The fat was in the fire.

The Declaration of November 21, 1974

J.H.: But Excellency, that declaration really was rude. Reading it again, one realizes its far-reaching consequence:

"We adhere with all our heart, with all our soul, to Rome, Catholic and Eternal, keeper of the Catholic faith and the necessary traditions to maintain this faith, to Rome Eternal, mistress of wisdom and truth.

"We refuse, and always have refused, to follow that Rome of neo-Modernistic and neo-Protestant direction which manifested itself clearly during Vatican II and after that Council in all the reforms which emanated from it.

"All these reforms have contributed to the ruin of the Church, to the ruin of the priesthood, the defacement of the sacrifice and sacraments of religious life, to a Teilhardian, naturalistic teaching in the universities, the seminaries, in catechesis, teachings which have their roots in liberalism and Protestantism which were condemned untold times by the magisterium of the Church.

"No authority, not even the highest in the hierarchy, can force us to abandon or diminish our Catholic faith, clearly expressed and professed by the magisterium of the Church for nineteen centuries. As St. Paul says (Gal. 1:8): 'But though we, or an angel from Heaven, preach a gospel to you besides that which we have preached to you, let him be anathema.'

"Is this not what the Holy Father repeats to us today? And if there seems to be a certain contradiction between his words and his deeds, as in the actions of his other departments, then we would choose what has always been taught and turn a deaf ear to the destructive novelties of the Church. One can profoundly modify the *Lex Orandi* without touching the *Lex Credendi*. A new Mass requires a new catechism, a new priesthood, new seminaries, new universities. A charismatic pentecostal Church is diametrically opposed to the eternal magisterium.

"This reform, which has its roots in liberalism and Protestantism, is poisoned through and through. It issues from heresy and ends in heresy, even if not all its actions are actually heretical. It is therefore impossible for any faithful and conscientious Catholic to adopt this reform and to submit to it in any manner whatsoever.

"The only form of faithfulness to the Church and to Catholic doctrine is, for our salvation, to refuse categorically the acceptance of the reform.

"This is why, without rebellion, without bitterness and without resentment, we continue our work of priestly formation under the star of the magisterium, convinced that we cannot render a greater service to the Catholic Church, to the Sovereign Pontiff and to future generations.

"This is why we strictly adhere to all that we have believed and practiced in the faith: morals, worship, instruction of the Church and for the Church, codified in the books that appeared before the Modernistic influence of the Council, in the expectation that the true light of tradition will dissipate the blackness which obscures the sky of Eternal Rome.

"By doing so by the grace of God, the help of the Virgin Mary, of St. Joseph and of St. Pius X, we are convinced that we have remained faithful to the *Roman Catholic Church*, to all the successors of St. Peter, and are the *fideles dispensatores Domini Nostri Jesu Christi in Spiritu Sancto, Amen.*"

Your Excellency, that "declaration" amounted to a declaration of war.

M.L.: I penned it, I repeat, under the influence of my indignation, scandalized as I was about the behavior of the two "apostolic visitors." But actually, this declaration becomes ever more fitting, ever more actual, and more true in the light of the bitter fruits of the Council.

In our days, obedience to the Catholic faith claims that the orders which, for the last ten years, have been organized and issued include the falsification of Scripture, the deterioration of Holy Mass, the adulteration of the catechism, permanent apostasy—in short, the self-destruction of the Church. They should not be obeyed, even if the Vatican pretends, but often without proving it, that these orders are coming from Pope Paul VI in person.

J.H.: It is easy to understand the emotion of the Holy See at the sight of this "declaration."

M.L.: Because many, like the Holy See, read it wrongly. The first lines are absolutely unassailable. And the rest stems from these first lines. May I repeat them?

"We adhere with all our heart, with all our soul, to

Rome, Catholic and Eternal, keeper of the Catholic faith, and the necessary traditions to maintain this faith, to Rome Eternal, mistress of wisdom and truth."

Make no mistake: It is no Luther, no schismatic, no heretic who could have written this!

Finally, so that there would not remain any doubt, I answered the abbot of Nantes, who pressed me to break with the Vatican:

"You should know that if a bishop breaks with Rome, it will not be me. My declaration said it explicitly and forcefully." I added: "Together with Pope Paul VI we denounce the new Modernism, the self-destruction of the Church, the stink of Satan in the Church, and we consequently refuse to cooperate in the destruction of the Church by the spread of Modernism and Protestantism, by entering into the spirit of reforms that are inspired by them, even if they come from Rome."

But I explained: "We think that, when the Apostle Paul reproached Peter, he showed toward the head of the Church the affection and respect which are the latter's due. St. Paul was 'with' Peter, head of the Church, who at the Council of Jerusalem had given precise directions, and 'against' Peter who, in practice, acted contrary to his instructions."

THE ACCUSATION

This is why I had no qualms when on February 13, 1975, I was invited to present myself in Rome to a commission composed of Cardinals Garrone, Wright and Tabera. Even less so since the letter of their eminences, asking me to come to see them, was extremely gracious. Anyhow, it did not allude at all to my "declaration." The cardinals wrote: "We have taken notice of the result of the visit paid to the seminary at Econe by His Eminence Monsignor Deschamp. We are grateful to you for having facilitated the mission with which the Holy See charged him.

"Now we would like to discuss with you some points which have puzzled us, and about which, among others, we have to render an account to the Holy See. Would you be free for this meeting the morning of February 13, at 10:00 a.m. in the quarters of our Congregation? We thank you in advance and assure you of our respectful and fraternal feelings."

I therefore accepted the invitation, not without finding it strange, in any case, that the report of Monsignor Deschamp, on which they wanted some enlightenment, had not been communicated to me. This was discourteous, contrary to common practice and even to simple good sense. But knowing the cavalier attitudes of Vatican II, I did not worry.

Oh, but it had been carefully planned to leave me in ignorance, to take me "cold," if I may say so, in order to make the trap which was prepared for me as escape-proof as possible.

Actually, on February 13, 1975, there was not an exchange of views, as I had been led to believe when I was invited. It was a tribunal which had me appear, as if I were the accused. And this tribunal wanted me to present myself without the opportunity to prepare a defense, since they had condemned me in advance!

Had one ever seen such a thing in the Church, except under the Inquisition? This is another fruit of Vatican II: it preaches so-called tolerance toward all ideas, but as soon as one opposes one of its aims, it is intolerance personified. Denying justice does not faze them.

Thus, instead of interviewing me in reference to the Econe seminary, as I had been promised, I was told only two words—to congratulate me, at that! And then I was attacked with a rare display of violence on the subject of my "declaration."

Cardinal Tabera, for instance, stated: "You have severed communion with the Church!" And Cardinal Garrone treated me like a fool.

I tried to defend myself. I stated once more that I respected, and would always respect, the Pope and the bishops. I explained that, in my opinion, it was normal to criticize certain Council documents, the reforms that were caused by them, and that it was wrong to say that such criticism amounted to a break with the Church.

Besides, all my actions since my ordination were a proof of my zeal to build the Church, rather than to tear it down.

We had a second "meeting" on March 3, but the case was closed. The three cardinals did not want to understand anything; they condemned me. I had the impression that I was facing a "kangaroo court." The proceedings which followed only strengthened my sad impressions.

For instance, I would gladly have obliged the demands of the three cardinals that our "conversation" be taped. Cardinal Garrone promised to furnish me with a copy of the tape, but when I claimed it, he refused. They even refused to let me have a typed transcript, but later on, such a transcript was given to the press, one whose authenticity was not at all unquestionable. I discovered in that document a great many "blanks." Are such dealings not reminiscent of the semblance of justice, as it is dispensed by dictatorships? At any rate, the verdict came down on May 6, 1975, in the form of a letter whose beginning surprised me a great deal.

First, the cardinals wrote that they acted "by express mandate of the Holy Father," of which, however, they did not provide any proof. Furthermore, they congratulated themselves that "the divergence of opinion among us has not prevented a profound and serene communion." This was a flagrant denial of the truth, since one of them, as I told you, had treated me like a fool. Finally, they said that my "declaration" was inadmissible from any point of view.

I had to read that sentence several times in order to believe it. Thus, in the eyes of the cardinals, the beginning of my "declaration"—I adhere with all my heart and all my soul, etc.—was unacceptable!

That was an enormity. The Vatican, which ridiculed the vow, as I reproached it in my "declaration"—that they were making a Rome of neo-Modernistic and neo-Protestant tendencies, of Rome Eternal, mistress of wisdom and truth—was now exacting blind allegiance to this Modernism and neo-Protestantism! All this to wipe out, with the stroke of a pen, the existence of the Priestly Fraternity of St. Pius X, and the seminary at Ecône.

I was ordered to stop everything and to dismantle everything. And this without the least care of what would become of the seminarians who had trusted me!

WITHOUT ANY FORM OF PROCESS

J.H.: I imagine that this censure provoked a profound effect on you. But maybe you thought of obeying it in spite of all?

M.L.: Frankly no! It was so unjust, so contrary to all canon law.

Therefore, I started a recourse with the Supreme Tribunal of the Apostolic Signature, which, in the Church, has a function similar to that of the courts of appeal in France.

I gave as a motive for this recourse certain evidences, such as:

That only the Sacred Congregation of the Doctrine of Faith is competent to judge the matter in question. In this case, the judgment of the cardinals' commission which condemned me had no authority at all, and therefore it is non-existent.

That the condemnation could not apply to anybody but the author of the "declaration" and that it was therefore inadmissible that the Fraternity of St. Pius X, all the professors and seminarians of Ecône who had nothing to do with it, should be adversely affected.

To dismiss 400 seminarians, 13 professors and all the personnel of the seminary two months before the end of the academic year, was this not inane?

This kind of recourse is usually studied a long time, sometimes months, even years. For me, five days were sufficient for the supreme tribunal to declare itself incompetent in the matter and to reject my recourse. It had been submitted the 5th of June and the decision was handed down on the 10th.

J.H.: It is rumored that those five days were a veritable moral martyrdom for Cardinal Staffa, the president of the tribunal.

That cardinal, who has the reputation of being a traditionalist, was suspected of favoring you. It was brought to his attention that he would be replaced if he expressed himself in your favor. One says, in any case, that he was the object of extreme pressures especially on the part of Cardinal Villot, who had forbidden him the least study of the recourse and prompted the order to reject it out of hand. This explains the hasty and surprising form of some of the arguments.

For instance, one of the arguments states that the condemnation by the three cardinals was "approved in specific form by the Supreme Pontiff." It is true that the cardinals acted on what they said was "a mandate by Paul VI." But there was never any proof of that "mandate" and, even less, of any "specific" approval. Had it happened, some document would have to be traced.

All this is very strange and has to be looked into. It leads to all sorts of assumptions.

One could assume that the Holy Father was badly informed about you by your opponents and that he let them act in his name. This finally put into question his own authority, even if he had not been kept informed of the proceedings. Had this been the case, the end would inevitably be that you either would give in or become every day more a kind of personal enemy of the successor of St. Peter. And you insisted the Pope should be asked to authenticate everything that had been done against you, including the trap laid by the commission of the cardinals, even if his own sense of Catholic morality inclined him to condemn personally the way all this was done.

Didn't he write you on June 29 concerning the judgment of that commission:

"We ourselves have instituted the commission which has kept us scrupulously informed about its work. Finally, we have completely and finally adopted the conclusions at which they arrived and we have personally ordered them to become effective immediately."

This amounted to furnishing *a posteriori* the famous "specific approbation" which made part of the arguments of June 10, which justified the rejection of your recourse. Surely, at the Vatican everybody let out a sigh of contentment.

But it has to be said that the skillful maneuver, of which the Pope might have been the object, so that the rupture between you and him should be irreparable, is only an assumption. But a few, rather troubling observations come to the fore which might well prove that the hand of Paul VI was forced. Thus, during a public audience on November 15, 1972, the Pope read a document on baptism in which he commented that to his regret the traditional exorcism ritual had been reduced to almost nothing in the new baptism rites. A few hours later, Professor Alessandrin, the spokesman for the Vatican, replied to a journalist who interviewed him with reference to the remarks by the Pope:

"One attributes to the Holy Father decisions which he certainly would not have approved, if he had been consulted."

Do you think, Excellency, that Paul VI, who is getting older and older, was "conditioned" by his surroundings, and that he had come to regard your insistence as a personal offense?

M.L.: I do not know anything about it. But, as I wrote to the abbot of Nantes, I am praying with all my might for the Holy Father.

How could he fail to be torn, he, the successor of St. Peter and the natural defender of tradition, who might be forced to swallow decisions and consequences of the Council which ended at the beginning of his pontificate? He has frightening responsibilities. And there is no doubt that dark forces try to weigh on his judgment more and more. He admitted it implicitly on June 29, 1972, with the remark which I quoted at the beginning of our conversation:

"We have the impression that through some chinks the fumes of Satan have entered the Temple of God."

VATICAN II
AND THE COUNCIL OF NICEA

I was bowled over when I read in his letter to me of June 29, 1972:

"The Second Vatican Council has full authority. It is even more important than the Council of Nicea."

That is an incredible statement. For Vatican II, I must repeat, was pastoral and not dogmatic, while the Council of Nicea was of capital importance and crucial. It condemned the Arian heresy, it affirmed the dogma of the divinity of Our Lord Jesus Christ, and it proclaimed the "symbol of Nicea," that is, the first part of the Credo of the Mass where the Son of God is declared consubstantial with the Father. To compare Vatican II to Nicea, and even put it above it, is unimaginable!

But that was necessary in order to condemn me. It was necessary that Nicea should not be anything and Vatican II everything, if one wants to brand as heretic and schismatic one who, to remain faithful to the dogma promulgated by Nicea, challenges the pastoral instruction elaborated by Vatican II.

What is really serious is the spirit which presided over it and which now can be found everywhere, as, for instance, with Dom Besret, who was the prior of the famous Boquen Abbey and who dared to write in his recently published book, *Du Commencement au Commencement*:

"That Jesus had the certitude that God existed was quite certain. But I do not believe that he was convinced he was the Son of God, to such a point that others took the shortcut of simply and directly calling him God."

Too bad that Dom Besret was a *peritus* at the Council of Vatican II, at the side of a bishop of France. And it is those "experts" who are listened to when one states that Vatican II was more important than Nicea—to condemn my seminarians, who believe in the divinity of the Son. To arrive at that, "the fumes of Satan had to infiltrate the Temple of God."

J.H.: In the letter from the Pope which we discussed, he also accused you of comparing yourself to St. Athanasius. He was not even the first to reproach you in this fashion, which implies that your pride is limitless. We should remember here that St. Athanasius was Pope during the time of the Arian heresy and was practically the only one to defend the faith.

M.L.: I have never said anything or written anything that might lead anyone to think I am comparing myself to St. Athanasius. The first time the name of this sainted bishop was mentioned concerning me was by one of the members of the cardinals' commission, Cardinal Garrone, who threw in: "You sound like St. Athanasius!"

The madness which has developed had led people to believe that I had aspirations to be "another Athanasius." As you can see, one resorted even to calumnies to turn the Holy Father against me.

SANCTIONS? NULL AND VOID

J.H.: We are now at a tragic impasse: You shrug off the condemnation of the Vatican and continue to ordain priests. And the Holy Father, whose authority is now in the balance, hardens his position. He suspends you from the divine office and extends the same sanction to your priests. This is for all practical purposes the schism feared by so many Catholics, including those who are most faithful to you.

M.L.: It would be an impasse if the sanctions laid upon me were legal according to canon law, and if, since then, I should find myself outside the Church. But this is not the case. All goes back to the first condemnation by the commission of cardinals, which I take to be null and void because there was no tribunal. Cardinal Garrone has admitted this publicly. Arguments are plentiful and some of them are decisive.

First, I repeat, since the process involving me was a process of faith, only one ecclesiastic jurisdiction is competent in the matter: the Sacred Congregation of the Doctrine of the Faith. Only this one could condemn me validly. But it will not do so, as everybody at the Vatican knows, because there is nothing in my dossier which could justify the least sanctions. One has never actually seen that congregation condemn a Catholic who held onto tradition. All it could do would be to congratulate him on his faithfulness to the Church eternal.

This is why one has fallen back on the creation of a cardinals' commission, who did not have to pass judgment according to canon law, but judged out of their own feelings, or the feelings which had been imposed on them.

It is true, the validity of such a commission might finally be justified by canon 1556, which says: *Prima sedes a nemine judicatur* (The one who occupies the highest position is not judged by anyone). But it is still necessary that the will of the Holy Father be authenticated.

To become convinced that such a document is necessary, one has only to examine the files of all those prepared and judged by similar commissions. Thus, in the dossier of Abbot Coache, who was condemned shortly after me, one can find the following passage: "On March 1, 1975, the special Commission of Cardinals, which the Holy Father had named by letter from the Secretariat of State, No. 265, 485 of November 4, 1974, assembled to re-examine, *ex novo*, etc. The decree here mentioned was submitted to His Holiness, Pope Paul VI, for his consideration. He approved it *re mature perpensa in omnibus et singulis* on June 7, 1975, giving the order to advise both parties immediately."

For me, nothing of the kind. In his letter of June 29th, the Pope indicated to me his accord with the constitution of the commission and its judgment. But this letter, *a posteriori*, is like an admission that the things were not done according to the rules.

Has it ever happened in canon law, and in any other law for that matter, that a decree, a decision, a law was made retroactive? First, one condemns, then one judges.

This is why the supreme tribunal of the Signature has rejected my recourse, because everything in this matter was arbitrary. So I started a second recourse on June 14, 1975. But here I did not even receive an answer. Cardinal Staffa, the head of the tribunal, had in the meantime received orders not to examine anything nor retain anything of what I might have written. This is what my lawyer told me.

J.H.: This explains the expression "savage condemnation" used by your friends to characterize the whole process.

M.L.: Doubtless. Now you can understand my serenity. As long as the first sanction that hit me is illegal, as long as my recourse—which brought with it the suspension of the penalty—is rejected without even being examined, all other sanctions, founded on that initial condemnation, are null and void.

J.H.: You are placing yourself on the plane of juridical quibble. Do you have to descend so low?

M.L.: Why does canon law exist? Is it not to prevent faithful priests and bishops from becoming victims of arbitrary decisions? If it is true that I am not a victim of the destroyers of the Church, why am I being so obstinately refused the only valid judgment, that of the Sacred Commission for the Doctrine of the Faith?

The law, like everything in the Church, should be at the service of faith. As soon as the law is in the service of destruction of faith, it must not be obeyed. The same holds for all the authority of the Church.

St. Paul, I repeat, told the Galatians in his time (Gal. 1:8):

"But though we, or an angel from Heaven preach a gospel to you, besides that which we have preached to you, let him be anathema."

9

I Am Not Worried

I SHALL NOT WILLINGLY HELP THE DESTROYERS OF THE CHURCH

J.H.: The more one studies the development of your relationship with the Vatican, the more one is convinced that the situation is hopeless, and at a dead end, at least for the moment.

As it does many Catholics, this pains me greatly. As far as I am concerned, I am close to being discouraged. I had actually hoped from our conversations that there would be some possibility for a few steps toward the Holy Father. I have imagined that your good will would elicit that of Pope Paul VI; I have dreamed of being an architect of reconciliation.

Unfortunately, as you will remember, I was at Econe the day the messenger from Rome, Father Dhanis, handed you the last message of the Pope, the seventeen-page typewritten letter, that "ukase" which enjoined you to deliver to the dioceses, wherever they are, the seminarians, the priories, the offerings of thousands of Catholics. I realized then and there that my efforts at reconciliation were in vain. For this ultimatum, which arrived on the eve of the Bishops' Conference at Lourdes, was intended to exhaust all possible attempts at rapprochement on their part. They who had been so worried about the recent opinion polls. Did they not triumph over you at the "wire," as the sporting expression goes? You had to suffer, but this suffering might become intolerable some day.

M.L.: Well, surely, it would be far from the truth if I said that I am not suffering from my difficulties with the Vatican or that I do not undergo anxieties. I am not different from other men. Every one, at certain instances in his life, recognizes this moral test. I imagine that our martyred saints knew it when they defended their faith in a hostile world, and we have to recognize it, perhaps even more intensely and painfully.

I am trying to follow their example. Recourse to prayer is a great help; it gives one courage not to falter.

I do not believe, to repeat your words, that they can triumph over the Catholic faith, over tradition, in the end. Should I fall, I am by far not the only one and somebody else will rise in the place where God has put me. It has always been like that in the Church.

In the meantime, I understand your desire for reconciliation. Eminent Catholics, writers and philosophers are ceaselessly at work about it. Some who even have the honor of having Paul VI's confidence seem to have dedicated their lives to it. They come to see me, they propose "ingenious" solutions. But in the final analysis, all these solutions consist of wanting me to abolish tradition and to eliminate the grain of sand, which is Econe, from the gears that were fashioned by Vatican II. So, even if I sadden my questioners, I have to reply "NO." No—I shall not make common cause with those who demolish the Church in handing over to them what belongs only to God, to the faithful and the everlasting Church.

These are the reasons why the situation seems to

have come to a dead end. But only in appearance. The time will come when the Church will triumph, as she always has. What are a few years, a few decades, in the face of eternity? As I told you: All you have to do is wait.

THE SUFFERINGS OF PAUL VI

J.H.: But your Excellency, if you suffer, even if you do not want to admit it, Paul VI is also suffering, and quite dramatically, it seems. I have had some intimations. Visitors recently received by the Pope found him extremely weakened, tortured by your "rebellion." They have the impression that you have cast a shadow over the end of a pontificate which wanted to bring to the world a brighter light and a greater and newer hope.

Some people even say that the central idea of the Pope was to make Vatican II the focus, the center of all religious ideas, for all aspirations of humanity. He must be terribly affected by the fact that you have put yourself "across" the path to achieve that "dynamic" to which he wanted to attach his name.

M.L.: I do not know if Pope Paul VI really has vowed this. But if he really wished it, it scares me, because it would be the compromise *par excellence*. It would, however, explain the persistence in trying to remove the obstacle which Econe represents.

We should remember the words of St. Pius X, when he was pressed by those who wanted "to open the Church to the world": "You want to open the doors of the Church to the world? But very few will enter and many will leave." What prophetic thought!

In any case, I have a completely clear conscience with regard to the moral suffering of Paul VI, even more so since I was able to measure it when he received me on September 11, 1976. But even if I am sorry for his sufferings, I cannot be persuaded to abandon the Catholic faith and to make myself over into a Modernist or a Protestant or atheist. All we can do is pray for Paul and ask God to enlighten him.

MOST HOLY FATHER, ACCEPT THE EXPERIENCE OF TRADITION

J.H.: Some people thought they could speak about this interview with the Pope. They said it was tempestuous and pathetic.

M.L.: People say all sorts of things.

J.H.: We are not going to disentangle the twisted account of those various, sometimes fantastic interventions made before the arrival of Paul VI. Maybe you would not even recognize them yourself!

M.L.: The essential thing is that the audience did take place.

J.H.: Is it true, yes or no, that before being received in audience, you addressed a letter which might be called a letter of repentance to the Holy Father? Some statements by some people lead to this assumption.

M.L.: In effect, I did write a few lines of which I do not have a copy. I simply indicated to His Holiness that if I was the cause of his suffering, I regretted it deeply. This, as always, holds true. But I have not made any pledge.

J.H.: Did you prepare for that interview?

M.L.: Of course! I have before me the notes which I jotted down on paper. I wanted to draw the Pope's attention to some points. Here is an example:

"Most Holy Father: The actions of the Holy See since the Council, and accomplished in the name of the Council, present a terrible dilemma for us. These actions rest on a doctrine which is getting farther and farther away from the magisterium which was solemnly confirmed by the predecessors of Your Holiness. Thus we find ourselves torn between fidelity to the eternal magisterium and fidelity to the Holy See and to your person."

I also wanted to tell him:

"The attitude adopted by the Holy See toward the world, that is toward non-Catholics and non-Christians, toward atheists and even toward the declared enemies of the Church such as Freemasons and Communists, is opposed to that attitude which the Church always had, which she kept for the defense of the faith and the life of grace. This attitude of false ecumenism and false dialogue is ruining the Catholic faith and the missionary spirit.

"That new spirit has its origin in the reform of the liturgy and in all the other reforms, like that of the Bible and of catechetical teaching. If we adopted this attitude, we would remove ourselves from the magisterium of your predecessors."

I wanted to develop the following points:

"The relations between the Holy See and the episcopate are now founded on principles which prevent the exercise of power by the Sovereign Pontiff. The resulting anarchy is of such dimensions that neither the Pope nor the bishops can exercise their personal authority of divine right.

"The rule of numbers is introduced into the government of the Church, contrary to the doctrine which was always taught.

"This alienation between the eternal doctrine and the actions of the Holy See, backed by the Council, has thrown the Church into such confusion that numerous faithful all over the world are deluged with novelties and changes, particularly in the priesthood and in the liturgy. Those faithful—much more numerous than one would think—together with clerics and bishops who do not dare to state those opinions publicly, are begging Your Holiness on their knees to authorize them to do what they have always done under such circumstances."

I wanted to conclude in this manner:

"Do not reject, Holy Father, these people of good will who are determined to serve God, the Church and the successor of Peter. The hour is grave. If Your Holiness forces upon us the choice between you and your predecessors, you will force us to choose your predecessors when it comes to the living Church through the magisterium and apostolic tradition, for we do not want to become either heretics or schismatics, but remain faithful to the eternal Roman Catholic Church."

This is what I had prepared and what I wanted to tell the Pope.

PAUL VI'S RAGE

J.H.: But the audience did not proceed the way you had imagined.

M.L.: Not at all. From the moment I was in the presence of His Holiness, I knelt down, only to see, when getting up, a tormented and feverish face. The look and the general attitude were not very encouraging. Before starting to tell him what I had prepared, I decided to wait out the storm:

"Holy Father, I am listening."

The reproaches which the Holy Father hurled against me left me stupefied. They showed how much the Pope had been influenced against me, how much my criticism of Vatican II had been interpreted as criticism of his actions.

"You condemn me," he said, for instance. "You assume that I am both Modernist and traditionalist. You incite the faithful against the Pope."

I hoped that, once the first assault was over, I could express myself at length and in the manner that I wanted, when he remarked: "Have you nothing to say? Speak up!"

I started to enumerate the points which I explained to you, insisting on the fact that I was not the head of the traditionalists, but a Catholic among other Catholics, troubled and torn apart. But I soon saw that, even if the Holy Father listened to me, his spirit was far from open to my arguments. When I got to talk to him about the seminarians of Econe, he interrupted me brusquely: "You don't form good priests! You have them sign an oath against the Pope!"

That was inconceivable! Who could have told him so? When we are teaching at Econe the highest respect for the successor of Peter, according to tradition! I was dumbfounded.

He continued: "What am I supposed to do when you condemn me? Resign? Is that what you want? To take my place?"

How much he had to suffer to put such questions to me! I suffered with him, for the Church.

I gathered my strength to say: "Oh, Holy Father, don't talk like that! I implore you: You have the solution to the problem in your hands. All you have to do is say a word to the bishops so that they give the traditionalists access to the places of worship. Think of the disorder in today's Church. Actually, we have twenty-three eucharistic prayers."

Paul VI lifted his arms: "Even more, even more!"

I continued: "If it is so, why not establish the Mass of Pius X in the houses of worship? Why not have priests experience tradition in their formation?"

Paul VI shook his head and replied:

"I cannot answer you. I have to consult the Curia first. I shall see, I shall think of it. . . . It is time to leave, but, before you go, let us pray together."

We recited the Pater Noster, the Veni Sancte

Spiritus and an Ave. Then His Holiness accompanied me to the door of his study. Alas, I was sure that our battle was to continue.

Cardinal Villot

J.H.: What is surprising in the interview is the Pope's allusion to the "oath against the Pope" that he said you require from your seminarians. Furthermore, as soon as you had mentioned it, the Vatican denied that the Holy Father had said anything comparable. In any case, Monsignor Benelli, who was present at the interview, stated that he had heard nothing of the kind. The thing is most unpleasant. It is a new element in what people have come to call "the war of lies" between the Pope's entourage and you. But who is lying?

M.L.: What do you want me to say? I am still smarting from indignation and that accusation. I asked the Holy Father if he could get me a copy of that oath. God knows, He will judge.

J.H.: Even those who know little Latin already have an idea of certain methods. The translation of the last letter the Pope addressed to you takes curious liberties with the original. One instance will do.

Speaking about the Priestly Fraternity of St. Pius X, the Latin document reads: *"Aequabiliter tibi praecipimus ut ea singula committas Sanctae Sedi."* This means literally: "We order you to consign them [the priories], each separately, to the Holy See."

But the translation given by the Vatican reads: "We also command you [with regard to the establishments] to hand them over, each one separately, to the Holy See." This is not the same thing. But someone undoubtedly wanted to neutralize the reactions of the traditionalists.

Many of your friends, your Excellency, see in all that the hand of Cardinal Villot. One of them said to me:

"This cardinal is more powerful than the Pope himself, for his skill triumphs over everything. And he puts as much eagerness into destroying his enemies as he did in conquering the high offices of the Church."

This manner of judging one of the highest-placed personalities in the Vatican makes my blood run cold, and personally I disapprove of it. Yet the cardinal seems to be driven by an insatiable ambition. Does he not fulfill thirteen functions? He is, among other things, Secretary of State, Chancellor of the Sacred Roman Church, Chamberlain of the Holy Church, Prefect of the Council of the Church's Public Affairs, President of the Administration of the Patrimony of the Apostolic See, President of the Pontifical Commission *Cor Unum*, President of the Pontifical Commission for the State and the City of the Vatican, President of the Cardinals' Commission for the Surveillance of Religious Works and Institutions, President of the Statistics Office for the Roman Church.

What do you personally think of Cardinal Villot, Excellency? Did he set the Holy Father against you—having everything prepared, everything ordered, and everything ready to obtain your condemnation? In short, is he a personal enemy?

M.L.: I prefer not to know; it does not concern me. The enemy of Econe is not Such-and-Such, at the Vatican or elsewhere. The enemy of Econe is liberalism, the destroyer of the Church. And as to the men who serve this liberalism and who aim to cut us down, these are not our personal enemies—they are only pawns of liberalism.

One must understand this: Our battle is not a confrontation between persons and characters. It goes well beyond: it is the battle of faith against error.

IS LIBERALISM A SIN?

J.H.: Destructive liberalism. Do you know, Excellency, whether your thought in this respect resembles that of any Catholics of the left, ecologists and others?

M.L.: I never have paid attention if my thought was on the right or on the left. The Church is neither on the right nor left—even though Our Lord has placed the elect on his right side and the damned on his left!

J.H.: Surely. But many who look at them see the elect on the left and the damned on the right! Whatever it may be, you pass for a "bishop of the right." And the appearances are not lacking for your enemies to make a show of them.

Thus the superficial eye that glances through the pages of *Liberalism Is a Sin*—one of the works for which you wrote the preface of the second edition—is rather shocked. The text is by Don Felix Sarday Sardani, a

Spanish priest who lived in Barcelona around 1880, and translated by the marquis of Tristany. This smells of the Inquisition and the aristocracy. But if one actually reads the book, if one strips it of the philosophical and literary trappings of the age, it says nothing that is different from what many Catholics of the left are saying; that is, that liberalism is the spirit of gratification, propagated to make the consumer society turn faster and faster every day. It *is* a sin.

We find ourselves here, it seems to me, at the nub of a question which has to be clarified. Accordingly, I have reread Maurice Clavel.

What is this "Christian of the left," this revolutionary of May '68, doing? He writes what you have been saying ever since the Council. What a contradiction, wouldn't you say, to denounce you as the representative of the utmost religious right?

On the other hand, I have read George Montaron. This director of *Temoignage Chrétien* [Christian Testimony], this outspoken Catholic socialist, writes in *Que qu'il en coute* [The Real Cost] of things that would scandalize you. But one can observe in his work, especially where he becomes introspective, a spirit that is akin to yours. Speaking of priests who give up their mission, he says:

"Other priests marry and present their new estate as a victory. The better to forget the promises made in their community, during their ordination and their years in the ecclesiastical life, they defiantly parade their marriage. But some of them consider the priests who remain faithful to their priesthood in celibacy and in the ecclesiastical structure as retarded in clericalism and as consenting victims of hierarchical oppression. They justify their personal failure with doctrinal explanations, and by doing so reveal themselves as 'perfect' clerics.

"Some people say that marriage for priests is the only answer to desertions. But the crisis is deeper. I, for my part, wish that the priests who chose celibacy would, with our help, remain faithful to it, so that they would not renounce greatness, and the occasion to be at the service of God and men."

This is followed by his analysis, which, if I am not mistaken, could be yours:

"The crisis of vocation is above all the crisis of the priest's personal identity. Everywhere in the world we see admirable and manifold generosities flourishing. Why, then, are the seminaries empty? Because those who are responsible do not know any more for what aim they form priests, and because those who have the desire to give themselves totally to the service of others in the priesthood do not know any more what role they are to play.

"In a world in which men and women need to project themselves, to tend toward the Infinite of God, the priest should be, more than ever, a man of God, the prophet who testifies by his word and deeds that God is alive.

"The consumer society needs prophets. If the priests are not prophets, we must not be astonished at the success of the various sects, of the adventures of the young in search of another world in drugs, the consumer society which gorges itself with rapidity and sex to escape the daily cross. Only the men of God can help us discover the true face of the Almighty."

What a beautiful plea for Econe, this word from an engaged Catholic who fights for socialism!

Thus, Excellency, if George Montaron and Maurice Clavel say that you are a bishop of the extreme right and the majority of Catholics repeat it after them, one can ask oneself if there is not an error of judgment and if words are not responsible for it.

You are using the same words, which are easily understood when they are posited only on the plane of faith and doctrine, but which, alas! take on quite a different meaning when one listens to them with a political ear. Thus, as always, back to liberalism.

You are opposed to liberalism because, for you, liberalism means the dissolution of morals, and the cash register, which fills the pockets of brazen capitalists. But many of those who listen to you simply think that, because you are against religious liberalism, you are also against political freedom, which means the power of money. Look how one little word can put you in the wrong.

Your ideas concerning atheistic materialism lead to similar judgments, probably because of the famous "primary anticommunism" phrase.

But, in fact, nothing is more opposed to a certain materialism than the true left, which more and more every day uses it for values which, when examined closely, are the same as those of traditionalism.

M.L.: I must keep on saying that I don't engage in politics—at least not in a partisan sense.

But there is politics according to the law of God, creator of the civic society and the family society. It is here that we cannot allow liberalism, which only wants to be liberated from the moral law, and ends in anarchy or dictatorship.

ST. THOMAS AQUINAS

J.H.: I would go even farther, Excellency!

I dare to state: You are, maybe, one of the first indications by which we can judge that our civilization, threatened from without and torn from within, will begin to defend itself.

I have a theory which will probably upset you: all cells, biological societies, living societies, all carry a hereditary gene that assures their stability, guarantees their identity and permits them to secrete adequate antibodies when they are attacked.

Now, when one considers the considerable and often determinant role played by Christianity in the Western world over the last 2,000 years, one may ask oneself if religion in society does not take the place of the hereditary gene, in the regulatory manner which I have in mind.

If this is the case, Econe might be one of the reactions of our society to the danger. No society can assure its survival except by saving its identity, principles, hopes and its eternal beliefs.

M.L.: Why did you think you would upset me?

J.H.: Because my theory is essentially materialistic. It reduces the religious fact to the range of instinct which assures the survival of the animal species. It makes of Econe a purely biological phenomenon.

M.L.: I see the things differently. I refer to St. Thomas Aquinas in his *Summa*, as translated by J. Chevalier. He says:

"The first rule is the Eternal Law which, in some way, is the reason of God. Natural Law is nothing else than the participation of Eternal Law in the creature of reason, participation appropriate to his nature and which his reason makes known to him."

If your argument came from such a source, it would probably be orthodox. Besides, it proves that St. Thomas has never been surpassed by any science, and that there was no need of the "spirit" of Vatican II to bring answers to the questions of our day.

May I remind you on this occasion that the seminarians at Econe strengthen their belief in the light of Thomism, whereas the new seminaries have relegated the works of St. Thomas to limbo in order to make room for the lucubrations of the "modern theologians"?

J.H.: My theory, Excellency, sins in another direction too. If it is true, it is opposed to the spirit of charity and love. It makes of our society an egotistical organ, concerned with the survival of its own identity. Wanting to defend the faith and defending the West seem to me to seek the squaring of the circle. A time will come when the imperatives of survival will make short shrift of the teachings of Jesus Christ: A civilization which offers the right cheek after a blow to the left is doomed.

M.L.: I don't understand how a Catholic can ask

himself such questions! It is not for a nation or a particular civilization for which that "gene" or that religious coordinator, as you call it, can assure survival and salvation, but for all of mankind.

Christianity, born under the Roman Empire, was not the savior of that empire. On the contrary, it has brought to the barbarians a spiritual dignity which that empire, in its egotism, refused them.

Catholicism does not identify itself with a people or a group of nations, not even if that nation or group of people has received the Good News before the others with a mission to spread it elsewhere in the world.

Here is one of the errors of Vatican II: Because the false spirits, destroyers of the Church, ranked Catholicism together with imperialism, the missionary zeal of the West was broken.

THE SEMINARY OF ECONE IS NOT A COMMAND POST

J.H.: Now, Excellency, we have come to the end of these conversations which doubtless have permitted many to understand better who you are and where you are going.

But where will all this end? Will you be able to continue your battle for a long time? At your age? Will you go deeper into schism, and consecrate a bishop so that your work may continue beyond your own life span?

M.L.: I have no intention of consecrating a bishop.

Indeed, I constantly repeat what I said in the Salle Wagram on October 4, 1975:

"The Econe seminary is not a command post. It does not aim to destroy other seminaries, nor is it here to fight the bishops.

"The seminary at Econe exists for the formation of priests, holy priests, so that one day the Pope and the bishops can rely on them, because only they will know the true faith, only they will know the true sacrifice of the Mass for which they have become priests, only they will know the sacraments and how to administer them."

Yes, that is what the Econe seminary is!

In the meantime, should I have to disappear before the Church triumphs, as she always does, I am not worried that there will be enough bishops in the world who will want to guide our seminarians. Even if he is silent today, one or the other bishop will receive the Holy Spirit to give him courage to act when the time comes. Hence, I am not worried. God is all mighty; what appears insurmountable to us is only a little thing in his eyes. If my work is God's work, God will preserve it and make it serve the Church for the salvation of souls.

J.H.: I take the liberty, Excellency, if you like, to conclude by recalling the opinions and the ardent vows of a great many traditionalists. These Catholics, I think, who have suffered much from the intolerance of Modernists, have seen in you the high conscience capable of establishing a stronghold in the face of regrettable experiences. But they are above all concerned with the unity of the Church and on this point they share the view of Father Congar: "A remedy MUST be found."

Your actions had considerable repercussions, as even your adversaries admit. As most of the faithful concede, even if they submit to Vatican II. You have rendered an immense service, you have permitted the Church to take hold of herself under the eyes of the bishops who have become more vigilant. Many parishioners feel it when they see that even priests of the avant-garde are now coming out against too much innovation.

Can His Holiness Paul VI, who in his own interventions so often censured so much of what you have branded as false, continue to misinterpret such service?

And is the new awakening of the conscience of churchmen not a sign that the time for mending might be near?

The Catholics of whom I was speaking thus hope that the Sovereign Pontiff and you will be able to overcome these most heartbreaking matters of dissension. They expect a public and forthright gesture from the Vatican concerning Econe and tradition, which can be understood by the faithful all over the world.

This would be a gesture which you could accept with confidence, so that this painful battle may finally cease.